Ultimate Success

Ultimate SUCCESS

Discourses on Spirituality

Swami Ramakrishnananda Puri

Mata Amritanandamayi Center, San Ramon
California, United States

Ultimate Success
Discourses on Spirituality
by Swami Ramakrishnananda Puri

Published by:
    Mata Amritanandamayi Center
    P.O. Box 613
    San Ramon, CA 94583
    United States

In India:
    www.amritapuri.org
    inform@amritapuri.org

In Europe:
    www.amma-europe.org

In US:
    www.amma.org

Dedication

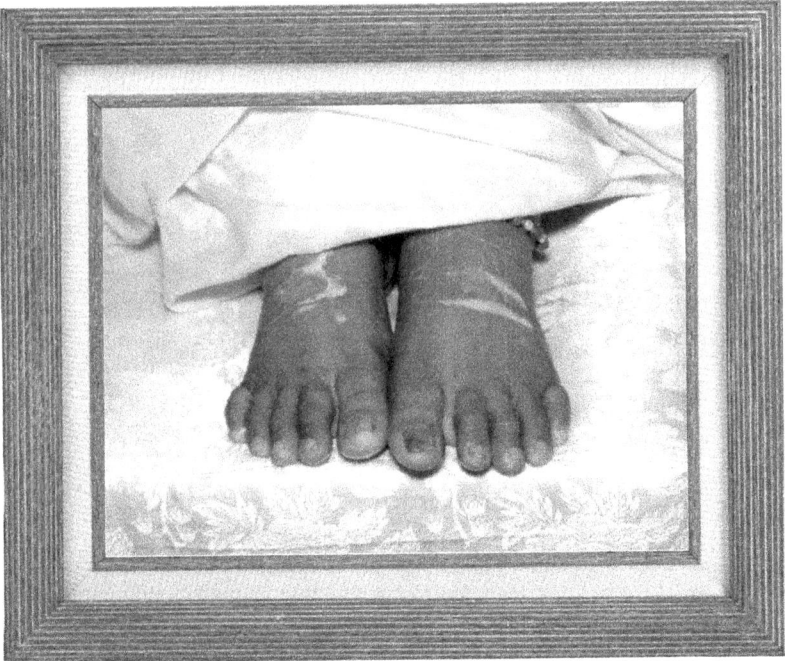

I humbly offer this book at the lotus feet of my beloved Satguru, Sri Mata Amritanandamayi Devi

Contents

Foreword

yo dhruvam parityajya adhruvam pariṣevate
dhruvam tasya naṣyathi adhruvam naṣṭameva hi

He who gives up the Permanent in pursuit of the transient loses the Permanent; neither does the transient remain with him.

—Ancient Indian saying

In the modern world, there are innumerable avenues to enjoy the pleasures of the five senses. Just as there is an information superhighway, there is a "sensation superhighway." From the most underprivileged to the wealthiest in society, everyone is bent on the pursuit of material pleasures, believing that the gratification of desire is the highest form of happiness the world has to offer.

Yet, we all secretly doubt that we will really be able to achieve all our desires and aims. We know that a billionaire may not have loving children, an Olympic gold-medalist may be suffering from mental stress, and a movie star's marriage may be on the rocks.

The truth is that nothing in the external world can provide lasting contentment. Of course, this does not mean that human beings should not pursue worldly happiness. However, while enjoying the pleasures of the world, we should be able to understand their true nature and seek that which will give us permanent happiness as well.

The only person who has fulfilled all his or her desires is the one who has transcended identification with the body, mind, and intellect and thus realized his or her true nature as the Universal

Self that is present in all beings as pure consciousness. When we have realized—through direct, personal experience — that there is only one "I," we understand that there is nothing more to gain in all of creation, and we are able to merge in the ocean of bliss that is our real nature and our final home.

If, on the other hand, we spend our life in pursuit of the temporary objects of the world, we will miss out on the permanent bliss of the Self, and in the end we will be without the objects of the world as well — at the time of death if not before.

Amma is a living example of a person who has achieved everything there is to achieve. From our present perspective, worldly objects may seem to offer the ultimate happiness in life, but to Amma, who knows Her own real nature, these objects are like peanuts. Once we attain the state of Self-realization, we can have anything that we want, but it is such a state of fullness that there is no room for desires — we do not feel that we are lacking anything.

Having had the good fortune of living with Amma for the past 27 years, I wanted to share some of the experiences I have had with Her, as well as the lessons I have learned along the way. The essays presented here analyze the possible pitfalls on the path to Self-realization as well as the infinite benefits we gain by that ultimate victory over our ego, based on the tradition of Vedic wisdom as well as my own experiences with a *Satguru* (True Master).

A devotee once remarked to me, "Amma is a riddle, wrapped in a mystery, inside an enigma." Not only do we not know who Amma is, we do not know who we are. In contrast, Amma knows from Her own experience that She and we — and all of creation — are one. That is why millions of people from all walks of life, from every race and religion and from every corner of the globe seek Amma's blessings and love. But Amma does not want us to remain in the dark. Amma's greatest wish is that all Her children, that is to say all living beings, will one day realize the supreme bliss of Self-realization. This is the ultimate success toward which one can aspire in life. Amma is the Ultimate Master who can lead us to That. May Her blessings and grace help all of us to attain this ultimate success.

Swami Ramakrishnananda Puri
Amritapuri
27 September 2004

Amma's Life in Brief

"Our God-given abilities are a treasure that is meant for ourselves as well as for the entire world. This wealth should never be misused and made into a burden for us and for the world. The greatest tragedy in life is not death; the greatest tragedy is to let our great potential, talents, and capabilities be underutilized, to allow them to rust while we live. When we use the wealth obtained from nature, it diminishes; but when we use the wealth of our inner gifts, it increases."

—Sri Mata Amritanandamayi Devi
"May Peace and Happiness Prevail"
Keynote Address, Closing Plenary Session,
2004 Parliament of the World's Religions

Amma was born in a poor fishing village in Kerala, Southern India, in 1953. Even as a small child, it was clear that Sudhamani, as She was then called, was unique. Without any prompting, She was deeply spiritual, and the intensity of Her compassion was remarkable. Because She was different, She was misunderstood and mistreated. She had a very difficult childhood and suffered a great deal.

From an early age, She spent most of Her time doing household chores. As part of Her work She had to collect food for the family cows. She would roam the local villages, gathering grass and visiting neighboring homes to collect vegetable peels and leftover rice gruel for the cows. At times like these, She saw many things that troubled Her heart. She saw how some people were starving while others held onto wealth sufficient to feed many generations. She saw that many people were sick and suffering

11

from intense pain, unable to afford a single painkiller. And She noticed that many of the elderly were neglected and treated harshly by their own families. Her empathy was such that the pain of others was unbearable for Her. Though just a child, She began to contemplate the question of suffering. She asked Herself, "Why do people suffer? What is the underlying cause of suffering?" And so powerfully did She feel the presence of God within Her that She wanted to reach out and comfort and uplift those who were less fortunate than She.

In many ways, it was then that Amma's mission began. She would share Her own food with the starving, and She would bathe and clothe the elderly who had no one to look after them. She was punished when She gave away the family's food and belongings to the poor, but Her compassion was such that nothing could deter Her.

People began noticing that there was something extraordinary about Sudhamani — that She was completely selfless, that She dedicated every moment of Her life to caring for others, and that She radiated a love that was unconditional and boundless toward everyone.

By the time Sudhamani was in Her early twenties, the universal motherhood that was awakened within Her made Her spontaneously embrace everyone who came to Her. She experienced each one as Her very own child, and people of all ages began to call Her "Amma" (Mother). Hundreds of people started coming each day to spend a few moments in Her presence.

Thus, Amma's *darshan*[1] took the form of a warm, loving, motherly embrace. Amma would listen to the sorrows of the

---

[1] The word "darshan" literally means "to see." It is traditionally used in the context of meeting a holy person, seeing an image of God, or having a

people who came to Her, consoling and caressing them. She also began teaching them about the true purpose of life.

Amma's first monastic disciples came to reside permanently by Her side in 1979. It was they who named Her Mata Amritanandamayi (Mother of Immortal Bliss). As more and more young men and women felt inspired by Amma's selfless compassion and began coming to Her for spiritual guidance, an ashram was founded. Thus in 1981, the construction of a few humble thatched huts next to Amma's family home marked the beginning of the Mata Amritanandamayi Math.

In 1987, in response to the calls of Her children throughout the world, Amma embarked on Her first world tour. Today, both in India and abroad, Amma is recognized as one of the world's foremost spiritual leaders. She spends most of the year traveling across Her native land of India, throughout Europe, the United States and Canada, Japan, Malaysia, Australia and more. Amma's compassion crosses all barriers of nationality, race, caste, gender, socio-economic status, creed, religion and health status. Wherever She travels, She greets every person who approaches Her with a motherly embrace, showing by example that unconditional acceptance and love are the foundation of service to others. In the past 30 years, Amma has physically embraced and blessed more than 23 million people.

Today, Amma's ashram is home to more than 3,000 residents. Thousands more visit the ashram every day from all corners of the world. Inspired by Amma's example of love, compassion and selfless service, ashram residents and visitors alike dedicate themselves to serving the world. Through Amma's vast network of

---

vision of God. In this book, darshan refers to Amma's motherly embrace, which is also a blessing.

charitable projects, they work to uplift those in need with shelter, medical relief, educational assistance, vocational training, as well as financial and material support. Countless people all over the world are contributing to these loving endeavors.

One of the most spectacular manifestations of this labor of love is Amrita Institute of Medical Sciences and Research Centre (AIMS), an outstanding non-profit 1,200-bed state-of-the-art hospital dedicated to health care excellence and improving the well-being of the community through preventive medicine, medical education, and research. At AIMS, even the poorest of the poor receive the very best high-tech medical care possible from highly skilled physicians and nurses in an atmosphere of love and compassion.

Most recently, Amma made international headlines in January 2005 when She announced that the Ashram would be dedicating 100 crores (U.S. $23 million) in aid to reconstruct houses throughout South India that were destroyed by the devastating tsunami in December 2004. Since the moment the tsunami hit, the Ashram has been focusing 100 percent of its resources toward relief work—providing free food, shelter, medical aid and emotional support.

Amma set up Her first educational facility in 1987 — the Amrita Vidyalayam (primary school) in Kodungallur, Kerala. Since then, Mata Amritanandamayi Math has established more than 60 education facilities throughout India including engineering colleges, computer institutes and a medical college; all of them imparting top-quality, value-based education.

Today Amma, who had very little formal education, is the chancellor of Amrita Vishwa Vidyapeetham, the youngest private university to be accredited by the Government of India, offering degrees in medicine, engineering, management, journalism and arts and sciences. Here the students imbibe the knowledge required for a successful professional career as well as to lead a happy and peaceful life.

More and more, Amma is asked to counsel not only individuals but also the global community of nations and faiths. Most recently, Amma addressed the Millennium World Peace Summit at the United Nations in New York (2000); the Global Peace Initiative of Women Religious and Spiritual Leaders at the UN in Geneva (where She was also presented with the 2002 Gandhi-King Award for Nonviolence); and the 2004 Parliament of the World's Religions in Barcelona where She gave the keynote address at the closing plenary session.

Perhaps the greatest expression thus far of Amma's love for the world — and the world's love for Her — was *Amritavarsham50: Embracing the World for Peace and Harmony*. Initially conceived of by Amma's devotees as a celebration of the 50th anniversary of Her birth, Amma, in Her own humble way, transformed the event into a prayer and a plan of action for the peace and happiness of the entire world. Over 250,000 people a day attended the four-day celebrations, including the president and deputy prime minister of India, a former U.S. senator, and many other political leaders, luminaries from all of the world's major religious traditions, business leaders from around the world, and of course Amma's devotees from almost every nation on earth. At the center of *Amritavarsham50* was, of course, Amma, doing the same thing She has done every day for the past 30 years — individually embracing, comforting and blessing everyone who came to Her.

As Dr. Jane Goodall said, while presenting Amma with the 2002 Gandhi-King Award for Nonviolence, "She stands here in front of us: God's love in a human body."

PART I

What is Ultimate Success?

Knowing others is intelligence;
Knowing yourself is true wisdom.
Mastering others is strength.
Mastering yourself is true power.
If you realize that you have enough,
You are truly rich.

—*Tao Te Ching*

CHAPTER 1

To Be Truly Successful

Everyone wants to be successful, but no matter how successful a person becomes, he or she still seeks something more. The manager of a department wants to become a senior manager, the senior manager wants to become a CEO, and the CEO wants to buy other companies. The millionaire wants to become a billionaire. The senator wants to be elected vice-president and ultimately president. Even after becoming president, he or she will want to become something more.

In this context, I remember an occasion when Amma met with the vice-president of a particular country. At the time, he was almost 75 years old and his health was failing. As he had worked his way up from the lowest position in his political party, everyone in the nation considered him a great success. He confessed to Amma that he had one final goal: to become president of the country — he felt only then would his life be a success.

No one considers his or her present condition to be completely successful. That is why there are so many seminars on becoming successful. For those who are already successful, there are seminars about how to become even more successful. There are even seminars on how to be successful in teaching others to become successful. Success is normally defined as something else or something more than what we have already attained. That is why we are constantly striving to acquire or achieve something.

Some people are after money while others are in pursuit of power or fame. And, of course, some people are dedicated to achieving noble goals. But when we define success as attaining any external goal, we will never feel truly successful. First, we may lack the qualifications to achieve that goal. If we are qualified, we may not get the right opportunity. Even if we get the opportunity, we may have to face many adversities. In addition, our goals will change with time and experience. By the time we achieve one goal, we may have a new definition of what it takes to be successful. Finally, we will always see someone else as more successful than we are.

However, from a spiritual perspective, everyone possesses the same inner wealth and has the same inherent potential to succeed. People with certain physical disabilities may never be able to succeed as an athlete. A mute may never succeed as a singer. A poor person without business experience may never succeed as an entrepreneur. A convicted felon can never hold public office. Yet all these people possess the same spiritual treasure as well as the potential to realize it and to be truly successful.

So what is real success? According to the ancient Indian way of life known as *Sanatana Dharma*,[2] there is one achievement of which it is said, "*Yal labdva naparam labham*," which means, "After gaining which, there is nothing left to gain." The achievement referred to is Self-realization. Realizing the Self means to experience that one's True Self and God are one and the same. This realization is real success. All other forms of success or achievement will be snatched away by death. On the other hand, firsthand knowledge of the Self will remain untouched by anything, even

---

[2] Sanatana Dharma is the original name for Hinduism. It means "The Eternal Way of Life."

death. Just as electricity is not affected when a bulb burns out, the death of the body in no way affects the Atman, which takes up a new physical body and continues with new life experiences. For one who has realized the Self, death is no more frightening than exchanging worn-out clothes for new ones.

When we say, "me," we are referring to our physical body and our personality, or our ego. We are ignorant of the Atman, which is our True Self — our essence. The Atman enlivens the body. Just as a vehicle runs only if it has gasoline in it, the physical body functions because of the presence of the Atman. This Universal Self, present in all beings, is also referred to as the Supreme Consciousness, God, or simply Truth. In a world of endlessly changing names and forms, only the Atman is changeless — it is the substratum of the whole of creation.

One who has this knowledge of the Atman is always content. Fully established in the Atman, or Self, such a person sees only his or her own Self everywhere and in everyone. As such, he or she will never feel more or less successful than someone else. When there is no second individual, who is there to compare oneself to? What is there to achieve?

Once there was a king who was getting on in years, and he still had no children to succeed his throne. It was an ancient custom of that kingdom that if the king had no children at the end of his life, one of the royal elephants would be sent out of the palace bearing a flower garland on his trunk; whomever the elephant garlanded would be named as the heir to the throne.

When it became clear that the king would die without having a child, he ordered an elephant to be sent out of the palace with a garland on his trunk, as per the custom. The elephant placed the garland around the neck of the first person he came across, which happened to be a beggar standing on the side of the road. Terrified by the proximity of the enormous elephant, the beggar turned on his heels and fled for his life. The king's ministers, who had watched the scene unfold, pursued the beggar and finally caught hold of him. They explained to the bewildered beggar that he was to be the next king and escorted him back to the palace.

After a few years, the king passed away and the former beggar was crowned as the new king. Though the ministers provided him with every possible luxury, he kept his old tattered clothes, begging bowl and walking stick in a golden chest in his bedroom. Several years into his reign, he had the idea to go back to his old life, just for a day, to see what it would be like. In the dead of night, he unlocked the golden chest and put on his old rags, took his begging bowl and walking stick and left the palace in secret.

Dressed as the beggar he once was, the king went to beg for alms. As the day wore on, he found some people would show compassion toward him and give him a few coins, while others would scold him harshly and treat him with disdain. The king was surprised to find he was unaffected by the way the people would treat him. When he had been a real beggar, he had been so happy when people had given him coins, and when they insulted him or scorned him he had seethed with anger that he dared not show. Now, when they gave him money, he was not elated, and when they scolded him, he did not feel upset.

Because the king knew he was really the lord of the land, the way others treated him did not make any difference to him. In the same way, *Mahatmas* (Great Souls) are unaffected by praise or blame, as they know they are one with God.

Amma is the perfect example of one who has attained this ultimate success. She neither needs nor desires to achieve anything nor to become something else. She is always content in Her own Self. That is why She is able to give so much. Even at the young age of three or four, the age when ordinary children are thinking only about their own toys and games, Amma was already helping the poor by giving them food and clothing from Her own house. Just think about what we were doing when we were that age. At least in my case, I can say that I was running around in dirty diapers and creating problems for my mother. But at this young age, Amma was already taking care of the elderly and sick people whose own family members neglected to look after them.

Amma's life also shows us that the ideal of a human life can be achieved irrespective of what we have or what we lack from the worldly point of view. We do not have to be born into a royal family like Krishna, Rama or Buddha. In Amma's case, in every respect, She started from scratch. She was born into a poor family in a remote, undeveloped village. Most of us, in contrast, are much more fortunate from a worldly point of view. Our material blessings may keep us content for a while (that is one reason we do not have a burning desire for Self-realization). However, this contentment can be lost at any time because it does not stem from within, just as the absence of symptoms does not necessarily mean we are free of disease. On the other hand, the contentment we get from realizing our True Self will never be lost under any circumstances.

Even today, Amma does not depend on others for Her happiness and contentment — it comes from within.

Some years ago, when Amma was in New Delhi, a meeting was arranged with the then–president of India. The annual festival at Amma's local Brahmasthanam Temple was in progress. Amma's darshan was to start at noon every day and go on until late at night with just a two- or three-hour break in between. Amidst this hectic schedule, an appointment with the president was scheduled for 9:00 in the morning. On the night prior to the appointment, the president's secretary called the local organizers and informed them that the president had to change the appointment to noon and asked if Amma could come then.

When this news was conveyed to Amma, She said that it would be impossible. Thousands of Her children in New Delhi were waiting to have Her darshan; how could She keep them waiting? At Amma's instruction, the appointment was cancelled.

How many of us would pass up an appointment with the president of our country? It would be such an honor and a chance for publicity and networking that nobody would want to miss it for the world. Through this incident, Amma demonstrated that She does not require any recognition from anyone.

People from all walks of life who are considered successful in their respective fields still come to seek Amma's guidance and blessings. Despite their so-called success, they still seek something more. Their worldly success has not given them what they really want: contentment and peace of mind. As long as we have the desire for something else or something more than what we already have, we cannot be considered truly successful. Only if we realize our True Self, which is omniscient, omnipotent, and omnipresent, will we feel truly complete and successful.

When a mother has something precious in her possession, she will definitely want to share it with her children. She will not keep it to herself. If we have excess food and we have eaten to our heart's content, what will we do with the rest of the food? Of course, we will give it to others.

That is exactly what Amma is doing. She is always full, content in Her own Self. Whatever She does arises from this fullness, whereas all of our actions emerge from the feeling that we lack something. Amma knows that, in truth, we lack nothing. We do not need to achieve wealth, power or fame to be successful. If we can remove the ignorance about our True Self, we can experience total contentment and bliss, regardless of our situation or circumstances in life. ❖

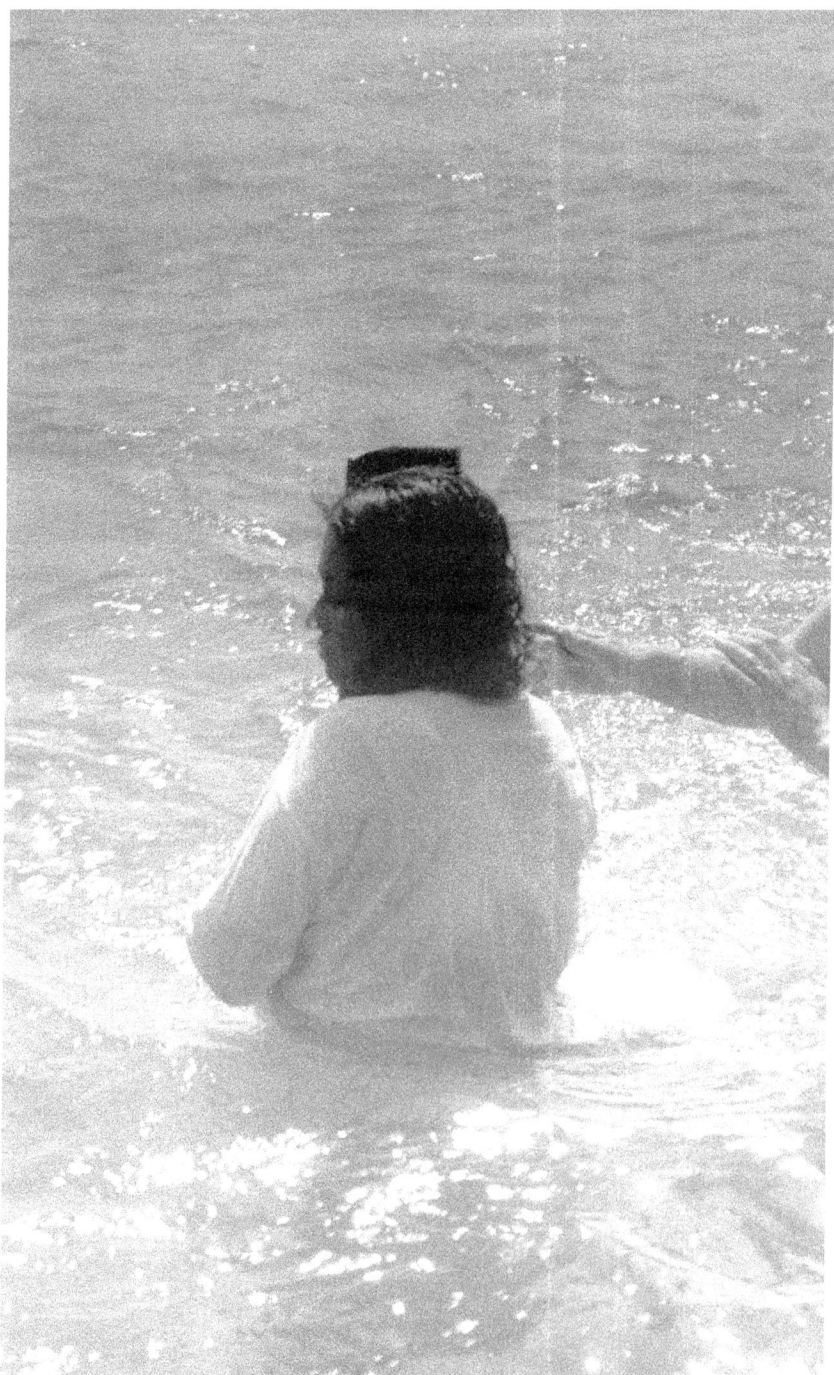

CHAPTER 2

What is Really Real?

When we look at the waves in the ocean, we see so much variety: small waves, big waves, gentle waves and fierce waves. Due to our limited perception, we see each wave as a distinct entity. When Mahatmas look at the ocean, they do not see the differences between the individual waves or even the difference between the waves and the ocean itself. This is because, essentially, the waves and the ocean are one — they are all the same water.

Similarly, Amma says, "There is no difference between the Creator and creation. Just as there is no difference between gold and ornaments made of gold (because gold is the substratum of all kinds of jewelry made of gold), there is no difference between the Creator (God) and the created (the world). Essentially they are one and the same, pure consciousness."

Our perception of reality is only relative. From our perspective, we may say that some delicious food is "simply divine!" Or, we may say, "That ice cream was heavenly!" In truth, we do not know what divine or heavenly really means.

Once there was a snail who was beaten up by two turtles. The police arrived on the scene and asked the poor snail, who was all black and blue, "Did you get a good look at those turtles that roughed you up?"

The snail responded, "How could I? It all happened so fast!"

For us, a turtle may seem to move very slowly, but from the perspective of a snail, the turtle may move with lightning speed. Our present perspective is similarly limited—we should not take it to be the absolute truth.

There is a story about a great sage called Ashtavakra. In Sanskrit, *ashta vakra* means "eight bends." He was given this name because his body was crooked in eight places. Despite his deformed body, Ashtavakra became a great scholar at a young age. His father was also a great scholar. One day, the king invited all the best scholars of the land to come to the palace and debate the scriptures. Whoever won the debate would win 1,000 cows with gold-plated, jewel-encrusted horns.

The debate began in the morning and lasted all day. As night was falling, Ashtavakra received a message that his father had defeated nearly all the competing scholars, but now he was on the verge of losing the debate. When the 12-year-old Ashtavakra heard this news, he straightaway went to the court to see if he could be of any assistance to his father.

Ashtavakra entered the king's court as the debate was reaching its climax. By then, his father's defeat seemed almost assured. When the scholars and the king saw Ashtavakra enter the court, all save his father burst into laughter seeing his deformed body and the cumbersome way Ashtavakra walked. Ashtavakra also began laughing uproariously. Everyone in the court was surprised, including the king. The king asked, "My dear boy, why are you also laughing, when everyone else is laughing at you?"

"I am laughing because the Truth is being debated by this conference of shoemakers," Ashtavakra calmly replied.

Knowing he had assembled the most highly reputed scholars in the land, the king asked, "What do you mean?"

Ashtavakra explained, "Seeing my deformed body, they laugh. They do not see me; they are judging me only by my skin. Therefore, I can only assume they are leather workers and shoemakers. My body is deformed, but I am not. Look beneath the surface. My True Self is unbending; it is straight and pure."

The whole court was stunned to hear Ashtavakra's reply. The king knew Ashtavakra was right — the debate had been a farce. Those debating the Truth could not see the Truth. He felt guilty that he had also laughed at Ashtavakra's appearance. He awarded the prize to the boy Ashtavakra, and the court was adjourned. That night the king laid awake pondering Ashtavakra's statement.

In the morning, the king's chariot passed Ashtavakra on the road. The king immediately got down and fell at Ashtavakra's feet, asking Ashtavakra to guide him to spiritual enlightenment. The night before, the king had addressed Ashtavakra as a boy. The next day, understanding Ashtavakra's greatness, he addressed him as his Guru. [3]

The king realized that even though his court had been full of scholars, they could see only the relative truth — they could see only Ashtavakra's body whereas the sage Ashtavakra could see within each of them the Supreme Self, which is the Absolute Truth.

The record of the dialogue that ensued between the king (Janaka) and Ashtavakra is called the *Ashtavakra Gita.* In it, the Master Ashtavakra says,

---

[3] In recent times, the word Guru has come to be used loosely; it can mean simply a teacher who is very good at his or her craft. In this book, Guru will be used primarily according to its traditional definition: One who is established in *Brahman,* or the Supreme Truth, and is guiding others to experience That.

sukhe duḥkhe nare-naryām sampatsu ca vipatsu
caviṣēṣō'naiva dhīrasya sarvatra samadarṣinaḥ

*For the wise person who looks on everything as equal, there
is no distinction between pleasure and pain, man and
woman, success and failure. (17.15)*

If we know gold, we can recognize all gold ornaments as different forms of gold. In the same way, if we know our True Self, we will see everything in creation as different forms of our Self. The problem with us is that we are trying to understand everything but our True Self.

Mahatmas like Amma see the same Atman everywhere. They do not discriminate between friend and foe, rich and poor, or between those who are kind to them and those who are cruel to them.

Recently, a man with a terrible skin disease came to receive Amma's darshan when She was giving a program in Madras. His appearance was so repulsive that everyone gave him a wide berth as he passed. Seeing his physical condition, the line monitors took pity on him and allowed him to go straight to Amma without making him wait in the line. Amma was not at all taken aback by his appearance. Taking him in Her arms and lovingly caressing him as Her own son, Amma asked him about his health and his living situation. He tearfully explained that he had nowhere to go; he had been trying to get assistance through various government agencies for several years to no avail. After listening to the sick man's woes, Amma summoned the *brahmachari* (celibate disciple) in charge of Her *ashram* in Madras and asked him to build a house for this man immediately through the ashram's free-housing project. Then She invited the sick man to sit by Her side, right in the midst of the local dignitaries who had come for Amma's darshan. Sitting next to Amma, the man's tears continued unabated, but they had become tears of joy. This man who had been abused and neglected throughout his life understood that in Amma's eyes, he and the dignitaries were of equal importance.

One day after She had given darshan for many hours, I asked Amma, "Why don't you look tired even after embracing so many thousands of people? How are you able to do this day after day?"

Amma casually remarked, "I am not doing anything." When Amma said this, I remembered a line from a *bhajan* (devotional song) entitled *"Amme Bhagavati"* that She wrote many years ago. It says,

Tan onnum cheyyadhe sarvam chaithidunna
Dina dayalo thozhunnen ninne

Without doing anything, You do everything.
O Embodiment of Kindness, I bow down to You.

When Amma replied to my question, She was speaking from the level of the Atman. When She said, "I," She was referring not to Her body but to the Atman, or True Self.

There is an interesting verse in the *Bhagavad Gita*, which says,

karmaṇy akarma yaḥ paśyed akarmaṇi ca karma yaḥ sa
buddhimān manuṣyeṣu sa yuktaḥ kṛtsna-karma-kṛt

The one who recognizes inaction in action and action in
inaction is wise among human beings.
That person is a yogi and a true performer of all actions.

(4.18)

Even though Amma is so active, She knows that Her True Self is not doing anything at all. This is seeing inaction in action. In our case, even when we are sitting still, thoughts continue to arise in our mind. Even to sit still, we have to make a conscious effort — that effort is an action. Superficially, we may seem to be without action, but we are still acting on different levels. This is action in inaction. Thus, the Mahatmas see the inaction in their action and the action in our inaction.

In the *Tao Te Ching*, it is said of the Master,

Things arise and she lets them come;
things disappear and she lets them go.
She has but doesn't possess,
acts but doesn't expect.
When her work is done, she forgets it.
That is why it lasts forever. ❁

CHAPTER 3

Choices & Awareness

Amma tells a story: A man from India visited his son who was living in the United States. When he reached his son's home, his son's wife received him with love and respect. She asked her father-in-law if he would like to have a cup of tea. The man said he would. Before going to the kitchen to make the tea, the man's daughter-in-law asked, "What kind of tea would you like? We have black tea, green tea, red tea, chamomile, lemon mint, and Chinese gunpowder tea."

"Just a cup of regular tea," the man from India shrugged. He had never heard about all of these variations of tea. His daughter-in-law left to make the tea. A few moments later, she ran back into the living room. "I forgot to ask you," she said. "Do you want milk in your tea?"

"Yes, please," he answered. "Okay," she said. "What kind of milk do you want? We have whole milk, two percent, skim milk, soy milk, rice milk, and powdered milk."

"Regular milk is fine." The father-in-law was losing his patience. He never knew a cup of tea could be so complicated. His daughter-in-law left once more. But hardly had she walked through the door when she turned around and asked, "Oh, I almost forgot. Do you take sugar?"

"Of course," said the father-in-law.

"Okay, I'll bring it in a jiffy. But what kind of sugar do you want? We have white sugar, brown sugar, turbinado sugar, *Equal, Nutrasweet, and Sweet'N Low.*"

At this last question the father-in-law lost his patience. "Oh, God! Do I have to answer so many questions just to get a cup of tea? For heaven's sake, I don't even want tea anymore. Can you please give me a glass of water?"

His son's wife did not lose her enthusiasm. She smiled saying, "Okay, what kind of water would you like — mineral water, sparkling water, vitamin water, or tonic water?" The father-in-law could stand no more. He stood up, rushed past his daughter-in-law into the kitchen and drank a glass of water from the tap.

In the modern world, we have so many choices even in drinking a cup of tea. The same is true for almost everything in our life. We can become a doctor or an engineer, a mechanic, a software professional, or even a monk. We can buy a one-bedroom house, a four-bedroom house, or a small apartment. We can buy a sports car, a station wagon, or a motorcycle. But when we find ourselves in a crisis or we meet with failure in our endeavors, we feel our only choice is to grieve.

In truth, even in such situations, we have a variety of choices. When we have a painful experience, we can choose to think that we have exhausted some of our negative *prarabdha*[4] or that we are

---

[4] Prarabdha refers to the sum total of experiences we are destined to experience in this life due to the results of our past actions. In the West, prarabdha is commonly called karma. The literal meaning of the Sanskrit word "karma" is "action," as in karma yoga, or the path of action. In order to avoid confusion and remain true to Sanskrit, this book will use the word "prarabdha" where the word "karma" would more commonly be used; the word "karma" will be used only according to its literal definition.

being offered a valuable lesson about the nature of the world. We can also consider the situation as God's will. Any of these attitudes would help us to accept painful experiences with equanimity. However, due to the mental conditioning we have acquired from our past experiences, most of us are not able to think positively when we are faced with a difficult situation.

We need to overcome our automatic or mechanical way of thinking and reacting. Our mind needs to be trained to respond and to act consciously — we have to cultivate awareness.

No one wants to feel sad, but at times, we all get down in the dumps. No one wants to get angry, but we all lose our temper. This means there is a gap between what we would like to be and what we are. By cultivating awareness and learning to respond instead of react, we can close this gap.

Due to the mechanical nature of our mind, we often make mistakes. We are not able to evaluate our own words and actions or the words and actions of others properly. If someone praises us, we think he or she is such a nice person. If the same person criticizes us later on, we will get upset or angry with him or her. In the moment we are confronted, we do not stop to think whether it is necessary to react with anger. One moment we are calm, and the next moment if someone comes and shouts at us, we will immediately shout back. It is only later that we will regret having lost our temper.

Once we train our mind to act and speak consciously, we realize that even when life fails to deliver us what we want, we have options other than to react out of anger or frustration. For example, if we are aware of the very first hint of anger arising within us, we will know we are about to become angry. This gives us choices: we can move away from the aggravating situation, or, if we remain in the situation, we can decide how much anger we are going to show. In such situations, we should remember the saying, "If you fly into a rage, be prepared for a rough landing."

When we look at Amma's life, we can see that under circumstances where most of us would have lost all hope, Amma's awareness gave Her the ability to respond differently. When Her parents denied Her love, instead of feeling pity for Herself, Amma thought, "Why should I seek to receive love? Instead, let me give love to others." When Her relatives and neighbors abused Her and criticized Her, instead of brooding over the way She was treated, Amma directed Her mind toward God.

Spirituality is the technique of increasing our level of awareness. Meditation, chanting, trying to follow the spiritual principles in our daily life — all these will help us to increase our awareness. If we can cultivate more awareness, we can overcome the obstacles that prevent us from realizing our True Self. ❖

CHAPTER 4

Dedication to Dharma

An important concept in Eastern spirituality is that of dharma. The word dharma has a deep and broad meaning. Simply put, it means both righteousness and duty. It also means performing the right action at the right place at the right time.

In order to adhere to dharma in our life, we need a thorough understanding of the nature of life and people. In a challenging situation or crisis, many people will forsake dharma or compromise their values. Though many such situations have arisen in Amma's life, we can see that She has never swerved even an inch from the path of dharma.

I remember something that happened recently that shows Amma's dedication to dharma. In March 2002, when communal riots broke out in Gujarat, Amma was in Mumbai. She was scheduled to leave for the earthquake-struck region of Bhuj, in Western Gujarat, where She was to inaugurate the three villages the ashram had reconstructed. But in order to reach there, She would have to travel through areas that had erupted in violence. Though they knew it was an important event, many people tried to dissuade Amma from going. Many members of the entourage went up to Amma, one after the other, and begged Her not to go, some out of fear for themselves and some out of concern for Amma. They said whether She traveled by train or bus, She and the group would be at risk. Since Amma was a state guest, officials from the government intelligence department provided up-to-date information on the security risks involved. They, too, discouraged Amma from making the journey. Amma was also told that the cabinet members and governor who had been expected to participate in the function might not attend for the same reason.

Finally, Amma put an end to all these requests and demands by declaring, "I have decided to go, come what may, and those who fear for their lives don't have to come." After this declaration, even people who hadn't planned on going decided to accompany Her.

The program was a huge success, and there were no incidents of violence. Later, Amma commented that the thousands of beneficiaries of the housing project had been eagerly waiting to meet Amma for a long time. Since they had lost everything, they did not have enough money to come to see Amma anywhere else. They also badly wanted Amma to bless their homes before they moved in. These were the factors that made Amma so intent on visiting them.

Amma always says that human life is attained because of the merit we have acquired by performing good actions in our previous lifetimes. Of course, we cannot choose where or when we will be born, whether we will be beautiful or ugly, short or tall, or who our parents will be. However, we can choose to be a good person. Even if we are kind and generous to others, we may get a negative response, but that should not prevent us from doing good work in the world. It is up to us to ensure that the blessing God has given us does not become a curse for us and for the world. For this, we need to make right use of our life.

We all have many responsibilities, burdens, and commitments in life. We need tremendous emotional and spiritual strength to live a righteous life. There are many situations where we might be tempted to give up dharma and compromise our values. Performing *adharmic* (unrighteous) actions may seem convenient at the time, but in the end, it will definitely have unpleasant consequences for ourselves and for others.

On the other hand, living a life of dharma and values forms a strong foundation for a rich and rewarding life. Not only is such a life very beneficial to the world, it can also help us become fit to receive God's grace, which is the most important factor in achieving both material and spiritual success. ❧

CHAPTER 5

Enlightened Action

In our life, sometimes we do the right thing and sometimes we do the wrong thing. When we do the right thing, naturally we take pride in it and take credit for our right actions. When we do the wrong thing, we tend to put the blame on others. When we interact with others, make a decision, or perform any sort of action, we usually take into account only the superficial facts and information available to us. So even if what we do seems to be the right action at that time, it may not be for the ultimate good, after all.

But there is another type of action that is beyond both right and wrong, and that action always leads to the ultimate good. This type of action is called enlightened action. Only an enlightened soul is capable of such actions. When a Satguru interacts with people, he or she knows their most subtle *vasanas* (tendencies), prarabdha and other factors. Whereas we can only perceive a person's physical actions — we cannot even be sure of what they are thinking or feeling. A Satguru is fully aware of the past, present, and future of whomever he or she meets. This awareness allows the Master to act in a way that will always lead to the best possible result for that person.

I remember an incident that happened in the ashram many years ago. One day a drunkard wandered into the ashram and started arguing with the brahmacharis for no reason. When we tried to calm him down and escort him out of the ashram, the drunkard started abusing us verbally. Despite our best efforts, the drunkard did not calm down but became even more unruly, so we decided to hand him over to the police. Before taking this final measure, we went to tell Amma about the situation. After listening to our explanation, Amma walked over to where the man was standing.

By this time, the man had thrown up several times and was only half-conscious. A putrid smell of vomit and alcohol hung about him. Looking at him with compassion in Her eyes, Amma lovingly called to him, "Oh, my son, what happened to you? Are you okay?" The man looked up at Amma with a blank stare and mumbled a few words. He wasn't in any condition to reply.

Some of the onlookers wondered, "Why is Amma spending Her precious time on this drunkard? This person deserves only a good thrashing." Someone even told Amma, "Please go to your room, Amma. We will take care of this man."

Amma paid no attention. She washed the drunkard's face with water and wiped all the vomit off his clothes even though he resisted a little bit. She took a hose from the nearby tap and ran water over his head in order to sober him up. Then She led him to a nearby room and laid him down on a mat.

The next morning, the man had sobered up and his mood had changed quite a bit. When he realized how Amma had taken such loving care of him, he was deeply touched by Her compassion and shed profuse tears of regret. That evening he went home. A few weeks later, he returned with his wife. During their darshan, his wife said to Amma through her tears, "Amma, you changed him completely. My children and I were on the verge of committing suicide because of his behavior. His drinking habit drove us into debt, and he would come home drunk everyday and beat us up. Now, he has stopped drinking completely, and he has even found a good job. By Your grace, not only my husband but our whole family has been saved!"

If the brahmacharis had turned the man in to the police — which seemed like the right thing to do at the time — not only would he have gone to jail and suffered even more, his family would have suffered the most. They may have even given up their lives. Thus, the "right" action from our point of view could have simply led to the death of several people.

Sometimes, our so-called "right" actions can be compared to the monkey who plucked the fish out of the fish bowl to save it from drowning. Similarly, we are capable of viewing things only from our own level of understanding, thus misunderstanding the ultimate good.

On the other hand, Amma, with Her deep intuition, perceived the best solution to the situation with the drunken man. She did not just consider that particular situation, but his future, his family's future, and the chain of consequences that could arise from the brahmacharis' intended course of action. An enlightened action may even seem to be wrong at the time; it is only later we will understand that it was the perfect action for that situation.

When Amma was in Bonn, Germany, about five years ago, a devotee in the question line handed me his question for Amma. The note explained that he was facing many financial difficulties, including debts, and that he had even lost his job. He was seeking Amma's help in resolving these problems so that he could support his wife and two small boys. His second prayer was that he wanted a baby girl.

"What a fool," I thought to myself. "How could he possibly take care of another child when he already has two children and a wife that he can't even feed properly? It's obvious he shouldn't have another child. What is the use of translating his letter to Amma? We don't need a Spiritual Master like Amma to prove his foolishness. I can do that!" Thinking thus, I started to give him my view on his situation.

While thus engaged, I felt someone tapping my shoulder. People often try to get our attention when we are translating for Amma. I ignored this call for attention, as I had not finished enlightening this man. Then the tapping became stronger and faster. I thought, "Who could have so much chutzpah to interrupt a senior swami?" Turning around, I saw, to my utter embarrassment, that it was Amma!

She asked, "What's the problem?"

"Oh, nothing, Amma. I was just answering his question."

"To whom did he ask the question?" Amma asked.

"Well, the question was for Amma, but...uh..."

"But what? Then why are you answering?"

I started fumbling for an answer. "Well, you know, I, uh, I just kind of, uh, you know... oh, no special reason, Amma. It was a silly question anyway."

I don't think my answer impressed Amma very much. She asked me to read the question to Her, and then, without any hesitation whatsoever, gave the reply: "Tell him Amma will make a *sankalpa* (divine resolve) for him to get a baby girl." Even though I had my own doubts and reservations about whether this was the proper thing to say to him, I translated Amma's answer, lest I end up losing my job of translating. He was happy, but I was unhappy. A doubt lingered in my mind about the answer Amma had given, so I asked Her about it later. Amma said, "The sadness in his heart from not having a baby girl is greater than the sadness and pain he feels because of his financial difficulties. If he doesn't get a baby girl, he will become depressed and may even take his own life."

For the next two years, Amma's program in Bonn was held in a different place, and this man did not come. The third year, however, we returned to the old hall, and the man came, this time with a baby girl in his arms. He seemed so overjoyed, and when he came for darshan, he explained that Amma's loving and assuring answer had given him a new lease on life. He had emerged from the cocoon of his sorrow with a clear head and found a good job that had helped him pay off much of his debt. The birth of his beautiful daughter had added to his joy.

Amma knew this devotee's biggest obstacle in life was his deep desire to have a baby girl, and once that was taken care of, all other problems would be resolved in time. By evaluating only the gross facts, anyone would probably have reached the same conclusion as I had about the wisdom of his having another child. Amma, on the other hand, could see the deep layers in his mind and had given an answer for his ultimate good.

Whenever Amma makes statements about the future, they always come true, no matter how unlikely they seem at the time. A few weeks after I first met Amma, I went to see Her at a devotee's house with one of my friends. We reached the house a little late, and Amma had already performed the *puja* (worship). When we went inside, we saw devotees sitting around Amma and eating. My friend stood some distance away and refused to come near Amma. He felt Amma should have waited to start eating until he arrived, since he had informed Her that he would be coming.

Amma called to him two or three times to receive Her *prasad,*[5] but still he refused. Amma told him, "Son, you won't get such opportunities with Amma for much longer. In a few years, people from all over the world will start coming to see Amma, and such opportunities will be very rare." When my friend finally agreed to approach Amma, he saw that while all the other devotees had already started eating, Amma had not yet touched Her food. In fact, She had even set aside plates of food for each of us. When my friend saw this, he regretted his mistake and asked for Amma's forgiveness. A few years later, he saw that Amma's words had come true.

The scriptures say that there is an authority to the words and actions of a Spiritual Master that is far beyond our intellectual understanding. Therefore, any judgment we make about them and their actions is bound to be wrong.

The following story illustrates this point: There were two blind elephants who couldn't agree on what humans were like. So they decided to try to understand what a human was like by feeling one with their feet. The first elephant felt a human with its huge feet and declared, "Humans are flat." The other elephant, after similarly "touching" another human, agreed and the problem was solved. Just as elephants lack the subtlety needed to understand a human with their feet, our minds are not subtle enough to grasp a Master's actions.

All the actions of a True Master are enlightened, just as any object made from sandalwood will carry the fragrance of the sandalwood tree. This is because Masters are established in Supreme Knowledge. As such, whatever they do will be for the best. Even

---

[5] Any item that the Guru has blessed is called prasad. Also, whatever is offered to the Guru or to God is sanctified and therefore becomes prasad.

though we might not understand them, we have to stay open to their advice and guidance.

In the *Bhagavad Gita*, Lord Krishna describes Supreme Knowledge as the most worthy thing to be gained by a human being:

rāja-vidyā rāja-guhyaṁ pavitram idam uttamam
pratyakṣāvagamaṁ dharmyaṁ su-sukhaṁ kartum
avyayam

This is the greatest of all knowledge, the king of secrets.
Supremely purifying, it can be directly experienced, and
yields everlasting results. It is also very easy to practice and
is in accordance with dharma. (9.2)

A person with Supreme Knowledge is always identified with the Truth, or Brahman. Under no circumstances will he or she suffer from any kind of identity crisis or be carried away by emotions or attachments. Amma is completely identified with the Supreme Truth, the inexhaustible source of energy and bliss. That is why She can sit for so many hours and yet She remains fresh, manifesting so much power. Though people from all over the world have been coming to Her with the same problems for the past 30 years, She never gets bored of listening, comforting, counseling and consoling.

The Supreme Truth is so precious. It is equally precious to be with one who is an embodiment of that Truth. Let us be aware of, and be grateful for, the blessed opportunity to be in the presence of a Great Master like Amma. ❧

CHAPTER 6

The Greatness of Humility

Amma says, "However powerful a cyclone is it cannot do anything to a blade of grass, whereas the huge trees standing with their heads held high will be uprooted." She also says, "If we are carrying the weight of the ego, the wind of God's grace cannot lift us."

Thus we can see that humility is very important. If we have the attitude of humility, divine grace will flow into us. But humility is a very rare quality in modern society. If we have done something great, how many days will we be talking about it to our friends? The first thing we will talk about is our own greatness. Some people will even boast about how humble they are.

If we want to know what real humility looks like, we need look no further than Amma. Though She has accomplished so much and is adored by millions, Amma never says, "I am great." Instead, out of Her humility, She tells us, "I don't know anything. I'm just a crazy girl." She never boasts about Her greatness. That is real greatness.

As you may know, Amma has personally consecrated 18 temples in India and abroad. Whenever She consecrates a new temple, huge crowds of devotees gather to witness the sacred occasion. As part of the consecration ceremony, Amma installs the four-faced statue that is the heart of the temple. At the very first Brahmasthanam Temple consecration, just before installing the image of the deity, Amma came out through each of the four entrances. With folded hands, She asked for the blessings of all the devotees assembled there. Seeing this, many of us were in tears. Here was someone who had blessed millions of people, and yet She was so humble as to pray for our blessings. Of course She did not need our blessings. She was seeking our blessings simply to remind us of the importance of humility.

In the *Tao Te Ching*, it is said,

> *The Master is above the people,*
> *And no one feels oppressed.*
> *She goes ahead of the people,*
> *And no one feels manipulated.*
> *The whole world is grateful to her.*
> *Because she competes with no one,*
> *No one can compete with her.*

Speaking at *Amritavarsham50*, Amma's 50th birthday celebration, Ms. Yolanda King, the daughter of Martin Luther King, Jr. (and an advocate for peace in her own right), said, "What I cherish about Amma is that She not only talks the talk… She walks the talk." As Ms. King so eloquently pointed out, Amma always practices what She preaches.

On Amma's 2004 North Indian Tour, Her one-night program in Durgapur ended at 6:30 in the morning. By 10:00 a.m., everyone had bathed and rested and was waiting near the buses for Amma to emerge from Her room so they could continue on the tour to the last stop in Calcutta. Several of the brahmacharis were standing near Amma's car. As they were often too busy during the program to go near Amma, it was one of their few chances to see Her. While they were standing there, a young man approached a brahmachari and began asking questions about Amma. He had not come for Amma's darshan the previous day because the length of the queue had intimidated him. He was just asking what makes Amma so special — why so many people wanted to meet Her and receive Her blessings — when Amma came out of Her room. The young man rushed toward Amma; She held him close and kissed him. She gave darshan to a few other devotees who were waiting nearby, and then She got into the waiting car.

However, She did not go far. The car drove only a few hundred yards to the site of the previous night's dining area where more than 15,000 people had been fed free of charge. The program had been held at one of Amma's Amrita Vidyalayam primary schools in the large open ground where the children play sports and exercise. Normally very tidy, on this occasion the grounds were a complete mess. Stitched teakwood leaves (which had served as plates) covered with bits of food were strewn everywhere. The garbage bins were filled to capacity and overflowing. A huge burlap sack of rotten potatoes lay on its side.

Amma's car parked next to the dining area. Amma got out of the car and, dressed in a shining white sari, began to clean up the mess Herself. All the brahmacharis and devotees present rushed to the spot and tried to dissuade Amma—after all, She had worked harder than everyone else combined the night before, and She had another program scheduled the very next morning. They knew that on the way to Calcutta She would have to stop and spend time with those traveling on the tour, and that evening She would have to receive the program organizers and local dignitaries. Why should She have to clean up this mess as well?

At the forefront of the protesters were the devotees who had been in charge of the serving the night before and the young man who had just met Amma for the first time. The devotee in charge of serving begged Amma for forgiveness, saying, "Amma, please don't do this. I know that I should have cleaned this area last night. Amma, please continue on your way and allow me to clean up the grounds."

"Amma is not placing any blame on you," She reassured him. "When Amma goes, all these brahmacharis and devotees will leave as well. While Amma is here, you have an army of helpers to clean up the grounds. That is why Amma decided to stay and help clean up. This way, the work will be finished quickly."

Amma proceeded to the sack of rotten potatoes, saying, "What a pity so much food was allowed to rot when there are so many who cannot afford even a handful of food to relieve their hunger." Then She called for a cart to be brought, saying, "None of you should touch these potatoes. They are so rotten you may catch a serious infection. One should wear protective gloves to handle such things." But then, when the cart was brought, Amma loaded the rotten potatoes into it with Her bare hands, much to the dismay of all present. The young man who had just met Amma was right next to Her and physically tried to prevent Her from doing the work. He protested, "Amma, You are the Guru; You should not do such things. Please, let me do this instead."

Amma was adamant that She alone would handle the rotten potatoes. Meanwhile all the swamis, brahmacharis, and devotees were walking back and forth along the grounds picking up teak-wood leaves and bits of food. Amma began making some room in the garbage bins by sorting through them and removing all the plastic. Mixed in with the organic waste were many empty plastic milk bags. Amma made a separate pile of these, saying that they could be washed and sold and the money used to feed the poor.

By this time, Her previously sparkling white sari was filthy with green and brown waste and stinking from the rotten food. Still, She was smiling, as radiant as ever.

Within 20 minutes, the grounds, which had been a disaster area, were almost pristine. Finally, Amma got back into Her car and instructed everyone except the brahmacharis to board the buses and get started. She told the brahmacharis to stay back and make sure the remaining garbage was disposed of and the grounds swept clean.

After Amma left, the young man who had just had Amma's darshan for the first time commented, "I had expected a guru who sits on a golden chair and gives advice. Never in my wildest dreams did I think I would see Amma cleaning up rotten food. There are so many people living in slums in Calcutta and all over this state (of West Bengal). If people would follow Amma's example of working for others instead of trying to get others to work for them, I think there would be no poverty left in the country. I have seen so many politicians making empty promises; now I have found someone who actually takes meaningful action." It seemed the young man's question — "What makes Amma so special?" — had been answered.

The boy had been expecting a guru. What he found was a Satguru. A True Master always teaches by example. Amma always says we should be ready to do any work at any time. If Amma did not put that teaching into practice, it might be hard to follow this instruction. But having seen Amma lead the way in doing the most distasteful work at the most inconvenient times, so many of Amma's devotees have been able to overcome their likes and dislikes and do whatever is required to serve those in need.

The year before, during Amma's 2003 North Indian Tour, Amma went to Her new ashram in Bangalore immediately after finishing a program in Mysore. When an elderly devotee approached Amma to perform *pada puja* (ceremonial washing of feet, as a demonstration of love and respect), She said, "Son, Amma has not even bathed. Amma left Mysore immediately after giving darshan. So, it is not proper to do pada puja now." But when She noticed the disappointment on his face, Amma relented. "Love breaks all barriers," She said. The devotee then washed Amma's feet with tears rolling down his cheeks.

After the pada puja, Amma started climbing the stairs leading to Her room. Suddenly, She stopped. Her expression changed when She saw the veranda. The marble floor was gleaming, perhaps owing to the fresh coat of polish. "Who built this?" She asked. The brahmachari in charge of constructing the Bangalore ashram came forward and prostrated before Amma.

"I don't need anyone's prostrations," Amma said in a serious tone.

"Amma, devotees from Bangalore built it as a token of their love for You," the brahmachari said in a feeble voice.

Amma retorted immediately, "Suppose they build a golden mansion as a token of their love, will you just watch quietly? Amma feels that Her children are not separate from Her. Although they built this room with their money, Amma feels bad because they spent so much money for Her sake." She continued, "I was born to humble fisher folk and led a simple life in childhood. Later, when told to leave the house, I stayed outdoors. I meditated under the scorching sun and lashing rains. I am not used to luxury nor do I want it. It is not appropriate for me to live in such a luxurious room when I advocate simplicity. What's more, I spend only

54

about three days a year here. It is not right to spend such a huge sum for an ashram." Her words were as sharp as arrows.

The brahmachari tried to explain to Amma that the flooring was not as expensive as it looked, but Amma did not heed his words, saying that She would rather sleep outside than stay in that room. At this point, Swami Amritaswarupananda said, "If Amma doesn't wish to stay in the new room, Amma may stay in Her old room. It has a cement floor." Amma relented. She walked into the room where She had stayed the previous year.

The devotees, who had never seen Amma in such a mood before, were taken aback. Some felt guilty, for they had been instrumental in building the new room. Others became very upset. Some were in tears. But all were wonderstruck by Amma's integrity and humility.

"Why did Amma reject the token of love?" they asked. "Is it wrong to offer our best to our Guru? After all, She deserves nothing less than the best. Why couldn't Amma have accepted the room? Millions of people all over the world revere Her as a Satguru and the Divine Mother. Who would have questioned Her right to live in this room?"

In the *Bhagavad Gita*, Lord Krishna says,

yad yad ācarati śreṣṭhas tat tad evetaro janaḥ
sa yat pramāṇam kurute lokas tad anuvartate

*Whatsoever the noble persons do, other people imitate.
Whatever they set up as the standard, that the world
follows.*

(3.21)

Amma's actions are so charismatic that we unknowingly start imitating them. Many of us prostrate before we sit on the floor or raise a book to our foreheads before reading. Many of Amma's children greet each other by saying, "Om Namah Shivaya." Don't we pick up these behaviors from Amma? Everything about Amma is so beautiful that we want to make it ours. If Amma were to live a luxurious life, we would want to do the same.

That evening, Amma went for a house visit. When She returned, hundreds of devotees gathered around Amma's car. They started pleading with Amma to stay in the new room. One said, "Amma, please forgive us and stay in the new room!" Another said, "Amma, we did it out of ignorance. We will not repeat such a mistake again. But, please, stay in the new room." A few women started crying.

Amma was unmoved. One devotee tried to use logic to persuade Amma to move into the room. He said, "All the money spent in building the room will be wasted if Amma does not stay in it. Nobody will use it in the future."

"Rent it out!" Amma exclaimed. "Use the rent money to help the poor. Amma has met many poor people with kidney problems who cannot afford kidney transplants. Such people need regular dialysis, which costs thousands of rupees. A kidney transplant costs at least 100,000 rupees. Even if they could afford the operation, they need to pay for post-operative care and regular medicines. How can the poor who cannot even satiate their hunger afford such expensive treatment? A person with a life expectancy of 80 years may die at the age of 40 because he or she cannot afford medical care. Aren't we all then responsible for that person's premature death? Money wasted on luxuries can be used to save many such lives."

The devotees accepted defeat. Amma then started walking toward Her old room. Before entering, She turned around to look at the faces of the devotees. Suddenly, there was a change in Her expression. Amma's face expressed love and compassion. In a soft voice, Amma said, "Yes," and started moving toward Her new room. The tension in the air dissipated, giving way to relief and joy. The devotees loudly expressed their gratitude to Amma.

Amma did everything She could to show everyone present that the money had not been well-spent. In the end, She acted out of Her overflowing compassion for Her children. She knew that their hearts were set on Her staying in that room and She did not want them to feel sad. Even while teaching humility, She was setting the ultimate example: Above all else, let our actions be guided by love. ❖

PART II

The Path to Ultimate Success

Follow then the shining ones,
The wise, the awakened, the loving,
For they know how to work and forbear.
Follow them
As the moon follows the path of the stars.

—*Dhammapada* (Buddhist scripture)

CHAPTER 7

The Body, Mind & Intellect:
A User's Guide

We all use many different instruments and machines in our day-to-day life to accomplish our tasks and meet our daily needs. However, if we do not know how to use these instruments properly, instead of benefiting from their use, we can even get hurt. If we want to receive the maximum benefit, the instruments we use must be under our control and should obey our commands.

Suppose we are driving a car and we want to turn left, but the car says, "No, I will turn only right," — we will be in trouble. We have all heard of science fiction stories in which the machines take control over human beings. We do not want such a situation to come true, for our life would become a nightmare. Unfortunately, a similar situation is already taking place in our life.

Our body, mind, and intellect are the instruments given to us to make the journey of our life comfortable. However, we often find that we are not able to use these instruments as we want to; rather, the instruments are using us. If at times we feel that our life is going poorly, the problem may be with the instruments that we are using.

In the West, people often think of the mind and the intellect as being the same thing. According to *Vedanta*[6], there are four inner instruments or, more accurately, four distinct functions performed by a single instrument. These are the *manas* (mind), *buddhi* (intellect), *chitta* (memory), and *ahamkara* (ego).

Manas is the seat of emotions. Whether we are feeling sad, angry, happy or peaceful, we are feeling it in the mind. It is also the faculty of doubting. Buddhi is the faculty of decision-making. This is the power that allows us to choose one thing over another. All our actions are prompted by the decisions of the intellect. Chitta is the storehouse of all our memories. Thus, it is the root cause of all our preconceived notions about the objects, people, and situations we encounter in our life. Ahamkara is the feeling that, "I am performing such and such an action, and I am experiencing its result."

Here, we are concerned primarily with the mind and the intellect. Vedanta tells us that the mind is nothing but a flow of thoughts. Just as a single tree cannot be called a forest, when there is only one concentrated thought or when there are no thoughts, it cannot be called the mind. Therefore, the mind undergoes a temporary death during deep sleep. When we sleep deeply, all our emotional turmoil comes to a halt. That is why we feel happy and refreshed after a good sleep. If we can retain that state of calmness during waking hours as well, we can resolve most of our mental problems.

Unfortunately, rather than the mind remaining under our control, most of the time we are under the control of our mind.

---

[6] Vedanta literally means, "The end of the Vedas." It refers to the Upanishads, which deal with the subject of Brahman, or Supreme Truth, and the path to realize that Truth.

The instrument is using us to do what it wants. Amma commonly gives the following example: As long as the dog is able to wag its tail, the dog can be happy and content. If the tail were to start wagging the dog, the dog could no longer get a moment's peace. Even eating and sleeping would become a challenge. Our situation is similar to that of a dog being wagged by its tail.

Amma says that if we get proper training to use the mind, our life will be more peaceful. Without a certain amount of peace of mind, we cannot meditate or do other spiritual practices with concentration. Control over the instruments of body, mind, and intellect is necessary.

If the mind is not under our control, regardless of how peaceful the setting, we will not be able to enjoy anything. At present, our mind is like a wild horse. Though nobody wants to become sad or angry, we invariably experience these feelings when faced with difficult situations. This is because we are not able to use our mind and intellect as we want to. If the mind and the intellect had been under our control, we could have faced the difficult situation with a calm and quiet mind.

We all have many defects in our mind such as impatience, jealousy, anger, greed, judgment, etc. The Guru creates situations to bring such defects to the surface, and then points out our mistakes. After we have become aware of the defect, the Guru will help us to overcome it.

In the early days of the ashram, when Amma introduced the daily discipline of getting up at 4:30 a.m. and meditating for a fixed number of hours a day, some of us were not happy, for we were addicted to sleeping long hours. We did not want to get up early in the morning. Some of us actually opted not to attend the 4:30a.m. meditation and *archana* (worship).

63

When Amma found out that some of us were not attending the early morning worship, She started attending. Many days She would go to bed only after midnight. However, to inspire us to wake up early, Amma would be there well before 4:30 a.m. ready to chant and meditate. When we came to know that Amma was attending archana having had so little sleep, we felt very ashamed and started attending regularly. Rather than giving the body the comfort of sleeping long hours, we were able to overcome our slavery to the physical body in this regard.

We used to get very emotional when Amma did something that displeased us, when She pointed out our mistakes or when She praised someone whom we did not like. We would go off somewhere to sulk or we might even argue with Amma. In the early days Amma did not pay much attention to our reactions. But after a few years, Amma started taking such outbursts seriously. When we reacted negatively to situations or to Amma's instructions or words, She would refuse to eat or drink. Sometimes She would even stand under the hot sun, in the pouring rain, or up to Her waist in the nearby pond. In this way, She would punish Herself for our mistakes. Amma told us, "You have all come to Amma in order to reach the goal of Self-realization. If Amma doesn't correct your mistakes, you will not be able to make real progress — Amma would not be doing justice to you. It is to help you grow spiritually that Amma has adopted such strong measures."

Later, She would lovingly advise us on how to face similar circumstances in the future. Then She would create various challenging situations to see if we were learning the lessons we were supposed to be learning. Through Her infinite patience and unfathomable compassion, we slowly started to become aware of our negative reactions and to repent for our earlier follies. Amma taught us how to put the instruments of the mind and intellect to good use rather than being used by them.

Amma is using Her body, mind, and intellect solely for the sake of Her children. Who can sit like Amma giving darshan hour after hour, day after day? By observing Amma's life, we can also learn how to make the best use of the instruments God has given us. Of course, we cannot imitate what Amma is doing. Yet, instead of just saying, "She is so wonderful," we should also try to learn the art of mastery over our body, mind, and intellect. Only then can we enjoy real peace and happiness. Otherwise, every situation in our life will disturb us.

We should not feel this is an impossible feat. There are many who forget about food and sleep while working to promote their business. Because of their commitment to attain the goals they have set, they are able to make the body obey their will. One devotee told me, "My son also forgoes sleep and food for many days — when he watches the World Series on TV!" Using another example, if a person's boss is angry or tough with them, they are able to control their own anger. They do not react. They know that if they react negatively, they will be fired.

Thus, we are able to control our body, mind, and intellect, even in difficult situations, if we are dedicated to achieving a particular goal or if we are very devoted to the object of our attention. We should extend this capacity to our spiritual practices and our behavior with others as well.

For Amma's devotees, it is our devotion to Amma that helps us to develop this capacity. Many years ago, when I was working in a bank, I would work overtime in order to earn extra money. When I resigned from my job to become a permanent resident at the ashram, all my enthusiasm for working faded away, and I became somewhat lazy. But seeing Amma's love for us, I wanted to help Her in whatever small way that I could. This allowed me to escape from my laziness and overcome my attachment to my own physical comfort.

When our love and affection for Amma overwhelms our attachment to the pleasures of our body and the desires of our mind, we are naturally able to bring our instruments under our control. ❖

CHAPTER 8

The Purpose of Life

Life is a journey, and this body is the vehicle given to us to complete that journey. It is a journey from the small self to the Infinite Self. That is why the scriptures say, "The human body is, indeed, the instrument to realize God, which is the ultimate purpose in life."

But in the West, human birth and the body are often not looked upon as serving such a high and noble purpose. In fact, even Shakespeare referred to life as, "a tale told by an idiot, full of sound and fury, signifying nothing."

Out of frustration, we may sometimes say that our life is useless or that we do not want to live anymore. However, suppose someone says, "I will give you a million dollars if you give me your hands and legs." We won't take them up on their offer because our body is so valuable to us. We may give one kidney, but not both, for our body is the most precious thing to us. When we will not give up even a part of our body for a million dollars, how can we say that our life is useless? Our life is definitely a gift, a blessing from God.

In the Hindu tradition it is said that before receiving a human birth, we have to go through hundreds of thousands of lives as lower forms of life, from a blade of grass to a tree, from a worm to the bird that eats it, to monkeys and various other animals. Even from the perspective of biological evolution, how many billions of years did it take for human beings to emerge on earth? From a single-celled amoeba to the fish in the sea, to reptiles and birds and finally monkeys and Neanderthals, how much labor has creation gone through to create the human body?

Even though it is so precious, the general tendency in today's world is for people to consider the body as nothing more than an instrument for enjoying the pleasures of life. Amma says that it is okay to enjoy worldly pleasures, as long as we don't become so enamored of them that we fail to realize our True Self. The Upanishads refer to such a failure as *mahati vinashti*, or "the great loss." Whatever happiness we experience in the world is only an infinitesimal fraction of the bliss of Self-realization. Actually, even this happiness does not come from outside us. When we fulfill a particular desire, our mind stops grasping for something outside, if only for a short time. At that time, we feel happy. But where does this happiness come from? When our mind briefly ceases its incessant efforts to acquire and achieve, we are able to dimly perceive the bliss of our True Self, as refracted through the darkness of our ego, attachments, and preconceived notions. It is this pale reflection that we call happiness. Most of us run after this reflection instead of seeking the source, which is our own Self. Mahatmas like Amma are never deluded by the reflection; they are totally content in the Self, which is the source and support of everything else.

It has been attributed to Albert Einstein that in his last days he said, "Sometimes I suspect that my life has been a waste. I enquired into the farthest of stars and forgot completely to enquire into myself—and I was the closest star!" Even though people whom we normally hold in high regard make such profound statements, we conveniently ignore or distort their words because they make us feel uncomfortable.

While enjoying the world, we must not forget the ultimate purpose of life. The body, mind, and intellect have been given to us as assets. In order that these precious assets do not turn into liabilities, we must learn how to use them properly for the achievement of the goal of human life.

In the *Katha Upanishad*, the body is compared to a chariot. The intellect is the charioteer, the five sense organs are the five horses drawing the chariot, and the mind is the reins that control the horses. The charioteer should know the destination as well as the means to reach it. He should also have good control over the horses. If the charioteer is qualified, he can reach the goal even though the vehicle is in poor repair. But if the charioteer is not qualified, even with a perfect vehicle, he may not be able to reach his destination.

Through Her example, Amma clearly shows us the proper way to use our lives in order to reach the ultimate goal of life: by using our body to help others, by using our speech to lovingly console others and by using our minds to cultivate good thoughts and prayers. Amma says, "The one whose legs rush to help the suffering, whose hands yearn to give solace to the sorrowful, whose eyes shed tears of compassion, whose ears listen to the woes of the distressed, and whose words bring solace to those in pain — indeed he is the true lover of God."

Amma says that She wants to put someone on Her shoulder and wipe that person's tears even as She breathes Her last. Even for those who hate Her, Amma has only words of love and compassion.

I remember an incident when two of the ashram residents had an argument. Actually, one of them was clearly at fault, for he had made a grave mistake. The other resident lodged a complaint with Amma, hoping She would kick out the guilty party. Amma first consoled the "plaintiff" resident and then called the "defendant." The "plaintiff" was sure that a brutal prosecution and cross-examination was about to take place. But to his dismay, Amma proceeded to instruct the other resident in a very soft way. After this unexpected outcome, the "plaintiff" appealed to Amma saying, "Amma, I don't see the justice in this."

To this, Amma only smiled and replied, "There is no justice in the court of the Master. There is only mercy and compassion. Justice will be obtained in the court of time."

We may feel that living a life that embodies all the divine qualities that we see in Amma is an impossible goal. No doubt there will be problems in everyone's life. But that shouldn't make us forget the goal of life. Amma has become what She is today not in the absence of problems but despite so many problems.

Unlike us, Amma had all the freedom to choose the circumstances into which She was born. When a devotee asked Amma, "Don't you feel sad thinking about all of the hardships you have undergone in your life?" Amma replied, "No, because I am the one who wrote the play that I am enacting now." Amma could have chosen not to be born. She need not have undergone all the hardships that She faced in Her life.

Amma chose such a life of hardship for Herself in order to show that in spite of all our problems, we can still cultivate divine qualities and ultimately realize our True Self. Even today, Amma doesn't need to give darshan day and night, answer our questions and doubts, or sing and meditate with us. There are plenty of people who would be happy to put Amma up in a five-star hotel for the rest of Her life. Of course, Amma would never think of doing that. Wherever Amma travels, unless She has an ashram there, She stays in the homes of devotees. Sometimes the house where She stays is very small, and there are only a couple of rooms for the whole group of about 15 members. Even the hosts tell Amma that they would gladly arrange a nice big house or book rooms in nice hotels, but Amma always refuses.

During Amma's annual European tour, She usually stays in the program hall between the morning and evening programs without enjoying the comfort of going to the house that has been arranged for Her. After the morning darshan, it may take an hour to go back to the house where She is staying and return to the venue for the evening program. Instead of spending the time traveling back and forth, Amma says, "I can use that time to give darshan to that many more people."

On Amma's 2002 U.S. Tour when She visited Iowa for the first time, the organizers had arranged a private plane to make the journey from Chicago easier for Her. They wanted to do whatever they could to reduce the physical strain on Amma, especially after a long night of darshan in Chicago. At first thought, it seemed a noble idea. Business executives and celebrities travel in private jets all the time; they are far less busy than Amma, and they don't spend 18 hours a day listening to the problems of thousands of people.

When Amma found out about this plan, She immediately asked that the flight be cancelled. She said that She had seen the suffering of millions of people around the world, many of them going without food, shelter, or medicine for lack of money. No matter who paid for the private plane, Amma said that She just

71

couldn't accept it, knowing that the money could have gone to help the suffering instead of for Her own comfort. Even today, Amma wears a simple white sari, sleeps on the floor, and eats only a handful of rice and a few vegetables. A beggar may also live on very little, but that is not real renunciation; it is out of compulsion or circumstances. Amma could have all the comforts of the world, and yet She takes so little from the world and gives so much in return.

Let us try to follow Amma's example as best we can. Instead of simply using our body as an instrument for enjoying the pleasures of the world, let us use it to selflessly serve and help others. Thus, our life will become a blessing for the world and ultimately lead us to Self-realization. ❖

CHAPTER 9

Ultimate Transformation

The rising sun, the full moon, the spring breeze, the lotus in bloom — though the development of technology and industry has had its impact on nature, the beauty and splendor of all these is undiminished. Even though these small wonders persist in every aspect of the world around us, we are unable to enjoy them as people did in generations past, or even as we could when we were children.

The incidence of depression and other mental disorders is skyrocketing. A schoolteacher in the United States related to me that every morning there is a line outside the principal's office — each child is waiting to receive his prescription medication for one or the other mental disorder.

We may think the world has taken a turn for the worse, and that is why our enthusiasm and energy has drained away over the past few years. In fact, it is not so much the world as it is our attitudes and values that have changed. What is needed is a total transformation of our vision of life and its purpose.

To illustrate the importance of individual transformation in the present-day world, I would like to share a report I read recently about the decline in society's values. A 1958 survey of high-school principals in the United States said the main problems among the students were:

1) Not doing homework

2) Not respecting school property

3) Leaving lights on and doors and windows open

4) Making noise and running through the halls

The results of the same survey 30 years later were shocking. In 1988, the students' main problems were rated in the following order:

1) Abortion

2) AIDS

3) Rape

4) Drugs

5) Murder, guns and knives in schools and colleges

6) Teenage pregnancy

If the same survey were taken in 2004, I would not dare to read the results.

Amma tells the following story. Once a father learned that his teenage son had been going to nightclubs. The father advised his son not to go to such places, saying, "If you go to nightclubs, you will see things you are not supposed to see."

In spite of his father's advice, the boy again went to a nightclub. The next day, he told his father, "Dad, I went to the nightclub last night. And I saw something that I was not supposed to see."

"What did you see?" the father demanded to know.

The boy replied, "I saw you sitting in the front row!"

Amma says the cultivation of good qualities like patience, kindness, and self-discipline should start with the parents. If the parents don't have these qualities, the children will follow in their footsteps.

Unfortunately, our minds do not naturally gravitate toward good thoughts and good qualities. As Albert Einstein said, "Science can denature plutonium, but it cannot denature the evil in man's mind." Removing the negativities from the mind is extremely difficult. It is not an automatic process like digesting food. We have to initiate the process consciously. Even if one is highly educated, removal of negative tendencies from the mind is not an easy feat.

We may wonder why this is so. When all else is equal, why does the mind tend to go downward and not upward?

It is because of our vasanas inherited from the past. When we act in a certain way — if it results in a pleasurable experience — it creates an impression in our mind that will prompt the mind to pursue a similar experience in the future. When we repeat an action many times, a strong tendency or habit is developed that becomes very difficult to break. In addition to the vasanas inherited from our previous births, we are creating new vasanas in our present life.

In the great Indian epic *Mahabharata*, Duryodhana, the eldest brother of the Kauravas, says, "I know very well what dharma (righteousness) is, but I am not able to act according to it. I know very well what adharma (unrighteousness) is, but I am not able to refrain from it." Duryodhana had the knowledge of right and wrong, but due to the strength of his vasanas, he was unable to utilize it.

Amma says that another reason our mind does not gravitate toward divine thoughts is because our parents were not having divine thoughts at the moment of our conception; they were having only lustful thoughts. This definitely affects our mind on a subtle level.

Ultimately, there is no use trying to figure out where vasanas come from. If we spend our precious time trying to discover their origin, we are like the man shot by an arrow who is more interested in who shot the arrow, what kind of tree the wood of the arrow shaft came from, and from which type of bird the arrow feathers came, than in the matter at hand — he must remove the arrow from his body and apply medicine to the wound. Similarly, we may not know how we got into a maze; it is enough if we find a way out.

One way of overcoming our vasanas is to take refuge in a Satguru like Amma. Many people undergo a remarkable transformation after meeting Amma. Alcoholics stop drinking, chain smokers stop smoking, cruel people become kinder, and many other bad habits or obsessions disappear.

At the end of my formal education, I wanted to become a doctor but ended up as an employee in a bank. Despite having a good job, my desire to be in the medical profession was very strong. Since I could not become a medical doctor, I aspired to become a sales representative for a medical supply company. I was obsessed with this career change. My father and friends advised me not to quit the lucrative bank job. They warned me that the medical representative job was not as good as my banking position. They told me that sales representatives are always waiting at the back doors of doctor's offices; they are at the beck and call of their customers. Still, I was not able to give up my unreasonable desire until I met Amma. After meeting Amma, this obsession disappeared spontaneously. Such transformations are common in the presence of a Mahatma.

That is why there is so much importance placed on meeting a Mahatma. Just as a person falling into bad company will take on the negative behaviors of the company he or she keeps, the association with a Mahatma will have a positive effect on our life and character. To say it another way, when we come into contact with bad company, we become bad; when we associate with a righteous person, we become righteous; when we associate with a Spiritual Master, we can become a spiritual person. The more receptive a person is, the greater will be the transformation. If we want to become more receptive, we can do our best to remember the Guru constantly, or as often as possible, and to follow the Guru's instructions with sincerity. We can also try to cultivate purity of mind by thinking good thoughts, trying to avoid bad thoughts and replacing our negative thoughts with positive thinking.

A few years ago, one of Amma's programs in Germany was held very near a bar. One evening, a drunken man stumbled out of the bar and into the hall where Amma was giving darshan. He asked a local devotee what was going on. She kindly and patiently explained that Amma was a saint from India and asked if he would like to receive Her blessing. He said he didn't care either way. Even though he was obviously very drunk and rambling incoherently, we brought the man for Amma's darshan. Amma took a lot of time with him, showering Her love and affection on him and showing concern for him in his intoxicated and disheveled state. We did not expect to see him again.

Three months later, when we were all back in India, he appeared at the Amritapuri ashram. He looked very little like the man who had stumbled into the program hall — his head was shaved, he wore clean clothes and a *rudraksha mala* (Indian rosary, made of seeds from the rudraksha tree) — but I recognized him as the very same man. I asked him what had happened to him. He replied that he did not know what Amma had done, but after the night he met Amma, he was completely transformed. Though his parents and friends had always told him not to drink so much, he had never been able to control his habit. He told me that on previous occasions, when he was very intoxicated, he had been treated badly and even beaten up by others. But that evening with Amma, he had received only love and kindness. After that, he had lost all interest in drinking. He told me he wanted to stay at the ashram now.

Even murderers have become great sages because of their association with a Realized Master. Many of you may know the story of the sage Valmiki, who composed the *Ramayana*. Before becoming a sage, he was simply a robber and a murderer living in the forest. After he met a group of Mahatmas, he was completely transformed. In a land of scholarly sages and saints, it was an illiterate, uncultured man of the jungle who became the author of the first great Sanskrit epic (24,000 verses), which is still read and enjoyed by the masses even after thousands of years. This is the miracle that an encounter with a Mahatma can bring about.

One other such example is that of Angulimala, who had taken a vow to murder 1,000 human beings and had already killed 999 when he saw the Buddha walking in the forest. Planning to make the Buddha his 1,000th victim, he began to pursue the monk. Though the Buddha was only walking at a leisurely pace, Angulimala found he could not catch up with him. Finally exhausted, he called out, "Oh, monk, stop!"

The Buddha replied simply, "I have stopped. It is you who have not stopped."

Confused, Angulimala asked the Buddha what he meant. The Buddha explained, "I say I have stopped because I have given up killing all beings. I have given up ill-treating all beings, and have established myself in universal love, patience, and knowledge through reflection. You have not given up killing or ill-treating others, and you are not yet established in universal love and patience. Hence, you are the one who has not stopped." Transformed by these words, Angulimala threw away his weapons, followed Buddha and became his disciple. Through performing good actions and sincere spiritual practice, Angulimala was even able to realize God. About Angulimala, the Buddha later said, "Whose evil deed is obscured by good, he illumines this world like the moon freed from a cloud."

I remember a related example in Amma's life. When Amma was in Her early twenties, there was a group of people in the neighboring village who did not like Amma's growing influence. They plied a village rogue, who had been in and out of jail, with alcohol and money to entice him to assault Amma. The rogue came to Amma's family home after midnight. At that time, either Amma's mother or father would usually watch over Her deep into the night while She sat immersed in meditation in the coconut grove in front of the temple. On this particular night, Amma sat for so long that finally Her father grew tired and went to sleep. Thus the rogue came upon Amma meditating alone, save for two dogs that were lying nearby. As he approached Amma, suddenly one of the dogs leapt up and sunk its teeth into his hand. Hearing the dogs barking and the agonized screams of the rogue, Amma opened Her eyes and saw the rogue cradling his bloody hand.

Though Amma clearly understood the rogue's motives, She went near him, told him not to worry and cleaned and dressed his wound. Then Amma told the neighbors, who had assembled after hearing the commotion, to take the man to his home without harming him in any way.

After this incident, the man who had meant to attack Amma was completely transformed. He even began ferrying Amma's devotees across the river free of charge.

Just being in the presence of a divine being creates a change in us. Through Her love and compassion, Amma is already bringing about this positive transformation in millions of Her devotees. Many of them have done bad things in the past, but because they were exposed to Amma's divinity, they have changed their ways and become righteous people.

In this way, Amma is not only helping millions of individuals, She is restoring the lost harmony in the family and in society. If we change, then slowly, the people around us will change. Others connected to them will begin to change as well. As Amma always says, we are not isolated islands but links in a chain. Whether or not we realize it, every action we perform influences others. Society is made up of individuals. When individuals change for the better, society as a whole will become more harmonious and peaceful. ❖

CHAPTER 10

The Desire that Eliminates Desire

We all have so many desires, the fulfillment of which makes us very happy. Unfortunately, many of our desires may lead to more and more desires. There is nothing wrong in trying to fulfill our desires, but we should remember that just because we desire something does not mean it will be good for us.

I remember a story about one of Amma's devotees that illustrates this point. He was a young man who had recently graduated from college with very good marks. His dream was to become a brahmachari and live in the ashram with Amma, but his family was very poor, and he wanted to help his parents and then join the ashram. Every time he came to Amma, he prayed that he could get a good job immediately so he could help his parents before joining the ashram.

Shortly thereafter, he was offered a job in the Middle East. It was a good job with a handsome salary. The only problem was that he would have to sign a binding contract stating that he would work a minimum of five years with the company. If he were to leave the job before completing five years of service, he would have to pay back all the money he had received from the company as salary. That was the deal they offered him.

He came to the ashram to tell Amma about the job offer. He told Amma, "They are offering me a very good salary. I have to accept this job."

Amma replied, "Why can't you wait some more time? You will get another job offer with better conditions." Though Amma had given him a direct hint, he did not want to listen to it. He was sure he would not be offered another job that would allow him to provide so much assistance to his family.

Thus, he accepted the job and worked for about two years. With the money he sent home, his parents were able to pay off all their debts. Meanwhile, their devotion to Amma became so strong that after getting out of debt, they sold their house and moved to the ashram. When the son heard the news, he was very upset because he had taken up this job with a five-year contract only for the sake of his parents. Even now, he is not able to come to the ashram, for he has not yet completed his contract.

If he had listened to Amma, he definitely would have gotten a different job, and after a short time he would probably have been able to stay in the ashram as a brahmachari. So we can see that sometimes desires — even seemingly good desires — can bring us trouble.

That is why it is said, "When you come to a Mahatma, don't ask for anything. Just tell the Mahatma your problems. They will give you what is best for you. Whatever a Mahatma does or asks you to do will definitely be for your spiritual growth."

I recall a story that illustrates how what seems to be a bad situation can be good for us and what seems to be a favorable situation can bring us suffering. Once a businessman from Mumbai came for Amma's darshan. He complained to Amma about how his business was failing and asked Amma to make a sankalpa to make his business flourish. Amma told the brahmachari who was translating for the man, "What he is going through now is for his own good."

Hearing Amma's reply, the businessman became desperate. He began pleading with Amma. "No, Amma! Don't say that. Please help me. Only if my business picks up can I be happy and successful."

To the brahmachari's great surprise, Amma began laughing. He could not understand why Amma was not showing compassion to this man, as She usually does to those who are distressed. It was only much later that the meaning of Amma's laughter became clear.

Many months later, this same man returned to the ashram. When he went for Amma's darshan, he began sobbing loudly. He explained to Amma that after he had returned to Mumbai, his business had begun flourishing. Around the same time, his younger brother joined the Mumbai underworld and started demanding huge sums of money from him. Initially, the businessman yielded to his brother, but when the extortion bids went on increasing, he refused to pay any more. Relations between the brothers soured, and the younger brother walked out of the house.

Then, unbeknownst to the businessman, the younger brother began to threaten the businessman's wife. Fearing the repercussions, she did not disclose this to anyone. The strain became too much for her, and she succumbed to depression.

The elation the businessman felt over the success of his business was dampened by the situation at home. The happiness he thought he would enjoy if his business prospered now eluded him. In desperation, he returned to Amma.

During darshan, he pleaded, "Amma! Please take away all my wealth. I don't mind being a pauper. But give me peace of mind. I have not been able to sleep for almost a week. Please, Amma, save my brother and heal my wife!" Amma was very compassionate toward him. She placed him on Her lap and caressed him lovingly.

A few months later, he sent a letter to Amritapuri. In the letter, he thanked Amma for having restored peace and harmony in his personal and family life. His brother and wife also became devotees of Amma.

In the case of the businessman, he believed that his floundering business was a curse, but later he realized that peace of mind was more important than money. If he had listened to Amma's advice in the first place, he could have avoided a lot of unnecessary suffering.

If we have many desires and expectations, we may find it difficult to meditate. We won't be able to sit calmly, for so many thoughts will trouble us. Amma says, "If we are doing spiritual practices and yet still desire so many things, part of the spiritual energy we derive from the practices will go toward materializing those desires. By indulging these desires, we are losing spiritual energy and our spiritual growth will be slow."

Amma is pointing out that we are wasting whatever spiritual energy we gain, just like a person who works hard throughout the day but then spends whatever money he or she earns on peanuts instead of buying something useful.

Now you may ask, "Swamiji, you say we should not have desires, but what about the desire to be with Amma? What about the desire to attain Self-realization?"

These desires are the only exceptions because they are helpful in spiritual growth. The desire to attain liberation or God-realization will take us to a state beyond all desires. In that state, we feel full and complete. The desire to be with Amma is not like a desire to own a big house or an expensive car or to become famous. If we get the house we wanted, eventually we will want a bigger house or a second house. Similarly, all worldly desires only lead to more and more desires, whereas the desire to be with Amma, or the desire for liberation, helps us to overcome other desires. Amma says that because of our attachment to Her, we are able to detach ourselves from so many other things. It inspires us to grow spiritually.

Amma gives an example. Suppose we have stepped on a thorn and it has gone deep inside our foot. If we want to remove it, we need a sharp object — even another thorn. Just as we use a thorn to remove another thorn, the desire for God or Guru will eliminate all other desires.

People can be classified into three types, depending on how they respond to their desires. The first type is called the *bhogi* or worldly person. This type of person eliminates their desires by fulfilling them. Suppose a person has a desire to go and see a movie. He or she would simply go see the movie and fulfill the desire. So that desire is eliminated. The next day if that person has the desire to eat pizza, he or she will run to the nearest Pizza Hut. Although it is common, this method of eliminating desires is very dangerous — it's like adding fuel to the fire. It is impossible to exhaust our desires by fulfilling them.

The second type is called the *tyagi*, or renunciate. Before attempting to fulfill a particular desire, the renunciate will ask, "Is fulfilling this desire going to help me grow spiritually?" If the answer is no — if fulfilling this desire is only going to increase his vasanas — this person renounces the desire.

The third type is the *Jnani*, or Mahatma, one who has already transcended all desires by realizing the Self. The Mahatma still eats and drinks, but for him or her, this cannot be called a desire. The Mahatma does so only to maintain his or her body. In the same way that they will speak the language of the land in which they were born and brought up, they may eat a particular food or drink depending on the culture in which they were raised.

There's a beautiful example from the life of Sri Ramakrishna Paramahamsa. Occasionally, he would ask for some kind of sweet, requesting that it be brought immediately.

Some people wondered, "He's a God-realized person and yet he has a desire to eat sweets? What is this?" Sri Ramakrishna explained to his devotees that it was difficult for him to keep his mind at a worldly level, as it was naturally drawn toward the state of *samadhi*.[7] He explained that whenever he thought of ordinary things like eating sweets or going to a particular place, his mind had to come back. "Before I let my mind soar into samadhi, I make a small desire such as eating a sweet or some other food, or I think of something else to do. Then my mind will come back to do it." Self-realized souls make such a sankalpa so the mind has to come back to the worldly plane. Just as an alarm clock wakes us up, these small desires or intentions are like an alarm clock reminding the Self-realized person to return to our level.

---

[7] Samadhi refers to deep state of absorption, a complete identification with the object of meditation. Whether his or her eyes are open or closed, a Mahatma is always established in the Supreme Consciousness. Many Mahatmas choose to remain inwardly drawn at all times, finding no reason to interact with the world, whereas a Satguru, while still experiencing that bliss, chooses to come down to the level of ordinary people in order to help them grow spiritually.

Amma says that when She sings bhajans, if She lets Her mind go, it is very difficult to come back from the state of samadhi. Nowadays, as there are always so many people there to hear Her sing, Amma makes a sankalpa before singing a bhajan that She should sing the whole song. To fulfill this resolve, Her mind will have to come back to sing each line of the song.

In the early days when Amma would sing a bhajan, She would often go into samadhi without completing the song. The brahmacharis accompanying Amma would continue singing the same verses over and over waiting for Amma to come out of samadhi so that She could tell us what the next song should be.

I remember a time when we were chanting the *Lalita Sahasranama archana* (1,000 Names of the Divine Mother) with Amma in the old temple. After chanting a few mantras, Amma would lose Herself in divine ecstasy. Sometimes She would laugh; sometimes She would cry; sometimes She would sit as still as a statue. When She emerged from Her ecstatic mood, She would ask us to continue chanting from where we had left off, but then She would lose Herself again after just a few more mantras. Usually it takes about one hour to complete the archana, but on this occasion, it took us five hours.

Amma has tried to chant the 1,000 Names of Devi by Herself on many occasions, but never once has She been able to complete the archana — She always loses Herself in samadhi. (Of course, there is no need for Amma to chant the archana, as She is one with the Divine Mother. It is only to provide an example for others to follow that She performs spiritual practices.)

In the early years, Amma did not travel much or give many programs outside the ashram, and She had not yet started any institutions or charitable projects. After She finished giving darshan to the devotees who came to the ashram each day and giving some instruction to the brahmacharis, She was free to spend several hours immersed in samadhi. Now, there is so much for Her to do and so many activities to guide that She has very little time to Herself. Thousands of people come for Amma's darshan every day; Her vast network of educational institutions and humanitarian activities is expanding all the time. Amma says that compassion is the natural expression of love. Out of Her overflowing compassion for us, Amma dedicates every moment of Her life to counseling, consoling and serving Her children, while never losing Her inner peace.

Thus, we observe that the Realized Masters may seem to have some simple desires, but it is really not so. If they have any desire at all, it is only to keep their mind on this plane in order to uplift humanity.

Through observing the selfless actions of the Realized Masters, we are inspired to follow their example. This will help us to transcend our selfish desires. Amma's brahmacharis are a good example. When we came to Amma, we all had many desires. I went to Amma to get a transfer to a bank closer to my hometown. Another brahmachari came to Amma to ask Her to bless him to earn good marks in his exams.

When Swami Purnamritananda (then Br. Sreekumar) finished his engineering degree, his father found a job for him at the Raman Research Institute in Bangalore. He had already been staying at the ashram most of the time, and as his parents and most of his relatives had become devotees of Amma, he had not expected his father to ask him to find a job. As much as his parents loved Amma, they were afraid of losing their son to a life of renunciation. They still harbored dreams of worldly success for him. So his father arranged for the job in Bangalore.

Going away from the ashram was the last thing Swami Purnamritananda wanted to do, but Amma pressed him to try the job for at least a few days. Amma and several devotees accompanied him to the railway station for a tear-soaked farewell. As the train rushed away, Swami Purnamritananda watched from the window as Amma and the devotees faded into the distance. He was sobbing and brokenhearted at the sudden separation. At that time, he could not bear to be away from Amma, even for a moment. The thought that he was being sent away for an indeterminate period of time was too much for him.

Without eating or drinking anything, he lay in the topmost berth of the train. Some time near dawn, he drifted into sleep. A little while later, he awoke with the sensation of somebody's hand stroking his forehead. When he opened his eyes, he could not believe what he saw. Amma was sitting next to him on the berth. He was not dreaming but fully conscious. He tried to get up but couldn't move his body or utter a word. Amma was silent as well, Her eyes glistening. A few minutes passed in silent darshan. Suddenly, Amma disappeared from his view. He closed his eyes and began meditating.

He spent the rest of the ride in loving remembrance of Amma, and he had to be shaken out of his meditation when the train reached its final destination of Bangalore.

A representative of the company was waiting for him at the station. The representative could not understand Swami Purnamritananda's moodiness. "Aren't you happy that you have this job?" the representative asked. "A job in the Raman Research Institute is the dream of many a young man," he explained. Swami Purnamritananda remained silent.

After a while he felt his behavior was not befitting the occasion, and he told the representative that he was feeling homesick. The representative was very loving and considerate. With motherly love, he prepared food and made him eat it, sitting by his side. He clearly felt Amma's presence flowing through the representative.

The next day Swami Purnamritananda began his duties at the institute. This job was what he had always dreamed of as a student, but now he felt only contempt for the position that had been bestowed upon him because of his years of education. The senior scientist soon took a liking to him and showered him with praise, but Swami Purnamritananda was unmoved. He passed his days there alone, silent and withdrawn.

On many occasions, Amma made Her presence clearly known to him through certain signs. During sleep, he would feel the sensation of flowers falling on his body; at other times, he would hear the jingling of Amma's anklets, the sweet fragrance that always accompanies Her would fill the air and Her voice would ring in his ears. Later, Amma told him that all these signs were to help him realize Amma is not confined to the limits of Her physical body and She is always with him.

Weeks dragged by in agonizing slowness. He received many consoling letters from Amma, yet he could barely bring himself to read the words. Many times he thought of returning to the ashram, but each time Amma appeared in a dream and told him to stay. He didn't want to disobey Her, so he decided not to leave.

One day, he unburdened his problem to the representative who had shown so much care and concern for him. That night, in the hope that Swami Purnamritananda would gain some peace of mind, the representative took him to a solitary place, a naturally beautiful area marked by steep hills and boulders. They slowly climbed up to the top of a huge rock and sat there talking about Amma. By that time, it was midnight. The representative lay down to sleep. Swami Purnamritananda closed his eyes and just sat there. A strange thought passed through his mind: "It is the body that is causing my separation from Amma. Therefore, let me destroy it." He got up, and making sure the representative was still asleep, he slowly moved to the edge of the rock, gazing down into the gaping crevice below. Then he closed his eyes and prayed for a few seconds, strengthening his resolve. Knees bent, he prepared to take the plunge to his death. But just as he began to leap, he was suddenly pulled from behind, and he fell backward. He looked around to see who had prevented him from leaping to his death, but the representative was still sleeping peacefully and no one else was in sight. He knew then that it was Amma alone who had held him back.

He sat up and meditated on Amma. Her voice resounded within him: "Child, suicide is for cowards. The body is precious. It is the instrument through which we can know the Atman. Many will be able to derive peace through it. Do not destroy it. To kill yourself is the greatest harm you could do to me. Overcome adversities. Be bold. I am with you." Finally, Amma gave permission for Swami Purnamritananda to return to the ashram.

Before meeting Amma, he had aspired to become an engineer in a top company. After meeting Her, even the job of his dreams could not satisfy him. His only desire was to be with Amma. This was a desire that eliminated all other desires and promised to lead him to a state beyond any desire at all.

The company of a Satguru is the best means to reduce or overcome our desires, even if our desires are deep-rooted. Sometimes the mere sight of a Mahatma is enough to help us overcome even our strongest desires.

One might ask, "I have come to a point where I have no more desires. I am satisfied and content with my life. If I don't have any desire or expectation, why should I perform any action? Why can't I just sit quietly?"

This attitude is simply idleness. We may not have any strong desire or ambition, but there will still be accumulated negative vasanas in us. If we do not work to get rid of these negativities, they can surface at any time and create problems for us. When our negative tendencies arise, they may prompt us to do wrong actions. That is why Amma asks all of us to do some selfless service and spiritual practices. Selfless service, service to the Guru and obeying the Guru's instructions in our spiritual practices and our daily life — all these will help to remove our accumulated negative tendencies.

As far as a spiritual seeker is concerned, it is important to overcome the negative vasanas, because they prevent us from realizing God. If we have negative tendencies, we will not be able to meditate properly, we will not be able to do our spiritual practices, and we will not be able to feel the presence of God.

What is the cause of these negativities? It is ignorance. We are ignorant of our real nature. Instead of identifying with the Atman, or Universal Self, we think we are the body, mind and intellect. We try to fulfill the desires of all these three, by fair means or foul. As mentioned earlier, when we perform such actions many times, it creates a vasana within us. Thus, ignorance about our true nature is the cause of all our negativities.

Of course, vasanas are not always bad. By doing selfless service, spiritual practices, and serving our Guru, we are creating positive tendencies that will slowly purify our mind and make us fit to receive God's grace.

Amma often says whatever we do repeatedly becomes a habit, and over a long period our habits form our character, and a good character is the fundamental quality one must have for spiritual progress. Sometimes we can see that a sudden transformation caused by meeting Amma does not last, and the individual slides backward into his or her old ways. When this happens, it is because the person did not take the initiative to imbibe Amma's teachings and to put them into practice in his or her life. Mahatmas can completely transform our lives, but whether or not that transformation is sustained depends entirely on how we respond to their love and compassion. Unless we are ready to walk a few steps hand in hand with the Master, the Master cannot lead us to the ultimate goal. ❖

CHAPTER 11

The Power of Habits

Amma says that the cultivation of positive habits is very important as far as a spiritual seeker is concerned because negative habits and qualities such as impatience, jealousy, and judging others prevent us from attaining peace of mind. Through Her own example, Amma inspires us to cultivate good habits. With the patience, acceptance, and love of a mother for her children, Amma helps us to overcome our negative habits; this leaves us free to enjoy life and pursue our spiritual practices with dedication and concentration.

Amma narrates the following story: Once a woman went for Amma's darshan. After embracing her, Amma asked the woman to sit by Her side for a while. The devotee had never had such an opportunity, and she was so happy to be so close to Amma for such a long time. She spent the rest of the day telling people of her good fortune and her blissful moments with Amma. The next day, the devotee went for darshan again and Amma again asked the devotee to sit by Her side. This time, the devotee was doubly happy and was overcome with tears of gratitude and joy.

After a short while, this devotee saw another woman coming for Amma's darshan. The devotee did not like this woman because she was jealous of her. Amma asked the second woman to sit by Her side, too. The first devotee was upset that Amma would ask this person to sit near Her. She felt increased jealousy toward the woman, and she even became upset with Amma. The first devotee was sitting in the same place as she had been sitting the previous day. The day before it had been a blissful experience for her, but on this day, it became a traumatic experience.

This devotee had been working overtime for an entire year just to save enough money to make the trip to see Amma and spend a few joyful moments in Her company. It was only after a long and arduous journey that she had reached Amma. She was amply rewarded by getting a chance to sit near Her (which is often difficult due to the huge crowds around Amma). But when she finally got her long-awaited opportunity, she could not enjoy the anticipated deep peace and joy; she became so agitated that she left the priceless spot next to Amma's side without being asked — all because of her habit of jealous thinking.

Just as we now find it difficult to practice good habits, after cultivating good values and good habits, we will find it equally hard to go back to our old ways. Several years ago, one of Amma's devotees who had directed a Malayalam movie gave a copy to Amma before it was released at the theatres, requesting Amma to watch it. The movie was not primarily a spiritual movie, but it integrated very good moral values. To make the devotee happy, Amma called all the brahmacharis and said, "Let's watch this movie."

Being prideful of the fact that I had lost all interest in watching movies, I told the other brahmacharis, "I don't want to see the movie. You can all go and see it." Amma did not insist that I come, but when the film was over, She called me and scolded me: "Do you think you are a great ascetic? Because you didn't do what I asked you to do, I am going to watch 10 movies with all the brahmacharis except you!" When She said that, I realized my mistake. Whether I felt like watching movies or not, I should always obey my Guru's instructions.

Amma did watch several more spiritual movies with the other ashram residents, but in accordance with Amma's instructions, I stayed away. However, as usual, Amma's punishment was tempered with sweetness. One day, She called me to Her room, and we watched a spiritual movie together.

By spending time in Amma's presence and doing our best to follow Her teachings and example, we will be able to cultivate good habits that are as difficult to break as our old bad habits once were. Once we have built up the forward momentum of good habits, it will become difficult to go back to our old ways. Thus we can harness the power of habits to propel us forward along the spiritual path. ❖

CHAPTER 12

Attitude versus Action

We must be mindful not only of the actions we perform but the attitude with which we perform them. If not done with the proper attitude, even acts of worship can pull us deeper into bondage.

In the great Indian epic *Mahabharata*, there are five brothers, called the Pandavas, who rule the country very righteously. One day Bhima, one of the Pandava brothers, was supervising the feeding of the poor. On this particular day, Bhima had also invited many *rishis* (sages) who lived in the area to attend. Bhima requested the rishis to supervise the feeding ceremony before eating. Lord Krishna was also present. The rishis were all sitting with Krishna when Bhima came and invited all of them to come and have their meal. The rishis were hesitant to go because Lord Krishna was there. But Lord Krishna said, "Go ahead; I will also join you."

When they all went to the dining hall, Bhima began to serve food and everyone started to eat. A great deal of food had been cooked that day, but the number of people who had come to eat was much less than they had expected. It was clear that a lot of food was going to be left over.

Bhima kept serving the rishis, even after they had eaten their fill. They said, "No, no. We don't want this much food," but Bhima continued serving, and when the rishis refused, he started to get angry and upset with them and even threatened them.

"What can be done with the excess food we have prepared? Take some more," Bhima insisted. "Otherwise, you will be disrespecting the king," he said.

Lord Krishna, who had been watching what Bhima was doing, called Bhima to come near him. Bhima approached Krishna reverently. Krishna told him that in the nearby forest, there lived a great sage. "I just met him before coming here," Krishna told Bhima. "He wants to give you some instructions. You must go and see him."

Bhima was very obedient to Krishna because he knew that Krishna was actually God. So he went to the forest as requested. Even from a distance he could see the rishi; brilliant golden rays radiated from his body. Bhima was greatly surprised. He wondered, "Who is this? Could he be another god?" Spellbound, Bhima walked toward the golden sage. As he walked closer, he started to smell something terrible. Even though Bhima could not stand the smell, he continued to approach the sage, for he wanted to pay his respects. As he moved closer, he realized that the foul smell was actually emanating from the body of the sage. Finally the stench became too much to bear and Bhima turned and went back to his palace. He went straight to Lord Krishna and politely asked him why he had sent him to the stinking sage.

Krishna explained, "One may be able bear the putrid smell of decaying flesh, but the stench of the ego is even worse."

Bhima asked Krishna what he meant.

The Lord explained, "In his previous birth, he was a great king; he helped his subjects a great deal. He would feed the poor, care for the orphans, and respect and revere the sages and saints.

But whatever he gave to someone, he expected them to accept it. If they didn't want to accept it, he forced them to. Though he was doing good work, he carried it out in an arrogant and egoistic manner. Because of the merits of the good actions he had performed, he was reborn as a rishi. Yet he had to suffer from the results of his arrogance in the form of that terrible odor.

"Likewise, if you force people to accept your charity even if they do not want it, you will have to face the consequences."

Thus, we can see that attitude is very important. Even though we may be doing a good thing, if we don't do it with the right attitude, it will not only fail to give us the desired result, it may even bring us harm.

There is another story in the epic Puranas that shows how good actions can have bad results if we do not have the right attitude. A great *yagna* (sacrifice) was performed by Daksha. Daksha was one of the *prajapatis* (progenitors) of humankind, which means he was supposed to take care of the human race for that era. Daksha invited all the gods to attend the yagna except Lord Shiva. He did not like Lord Shiva because of his appearance. With his matted hair, ash all over his body, snakes around his neck, just a piece of animal hide around his waist and a begging bowl in his hand, Daksha thought Shiva looked more like a wandering monk than a god. The fact that Daksha's daughter, Sati, loved Shiva and had even married him made Daksha dislike Shiva all the more. To add insult to injury, recently Daksha had entered an assembly of *devas* (celestial beings) and sages, and everyone had risen to show respect to him. Only Shiva, who as his son-in-law was supposed to respect him, had not gotten up from his seat. In retaliation, Daksha was performing this great yagna without inviting Shiva.

When they found out Daksha had not invited Lord Shiva to the yagna, his ministers and other celestial beings advised him that Shiva was the greatest of all gods, so Daksha should show proper respect by inviting him to the yagna. Moreover, Daksha's ministers reminded him, Shiva is the first and foremost Guru in the lineage of all the Great Masters. According to Indian tradition, no work or worship can begin without first invoking the Guru, followed by Ganesha. But Daksha was adamant.

Daksha's daughter Sati came to know of the great yagna and asked Lord Shiva's permission to attend. Shiva replied, "He is going to abuse you because you are my wife. He will ridicule you and treat you with disdain. Moreover, he has not invited you. It is better for you not to go."

Sati responded, "I do not need an invitation from him. He is, after all, my father. One doesn't need an invitation to go to one's father's house. Besides, I want to convince him to give you due recognition."

Sati attended the yagna against Shiva's wishes. She entered the palace where all the gods and celestial beings were seated around the massive bonfire lit for the purpose of the yagna.

As predicted by Lord Shiva, when Daksha saw Sati he showed her scant respect. He started verbally abusing Lord Shiva, saying, "Your husband is nothing more than a beggar and a madman. Is it because he has only a begging bowl to his name that he loiters in the graveyard? He is fit only for the company of the dead." Daksha went on abusing her husband, and finally Sati could bear no more. By her yogic powers, Sati brought forth fire from within herself, giving up her body.

When Shiva came to know that Sati had given up her body, He was furious. He called forth his army, sending them to the site of the yagna. They killed Daksha and destroyed the entire yagna. Fearing Shiva's wrath, all the other devas fled for their lives.

Later, out of his compassion, Shiva brought Daksha back to life, replacing his severed head with that of a goat. Then Daksha realized his mistake and prayed to Shiva for forgiveness. Though he had been conducting a great yagna — which was considered among the most righteous of actions — because of his wrong attitude, it had ended in war and destruction.[8] Even an act of worship, devoid of humility and devotion, can bring only calamity.

Now let us take the example of the Mahabharata War. Because the actions of the unrighteous Kauravas were destroying the harmony in the country, after exhausting all other methods of diplomacy Lord Krishna finally advised Arjuna and the righteous Pandavas to wage war against them. In this war, following the instructions of Lord Krishna, Arjuna killed hundreds of thousands of people — including his close relatives — in order to restore righteousness and harmony to the world. Even though Arjuna did not want to fight in the war, he surrendered to Lord Krishna and obeyed Him implicitly. Thus while Daksha's yagna became a war,

---

[8] There is a great deal of symbolism in this story. The marriage of Sati with Shiva actually represents her acceptance of a Spiritual Master, which is often despised by parents who have worldly expectations for their children. Sati's self-sacrifice also teaches us that once we dedicate our life to the pursuit of the spiritual goal, we should not remain attached to anything. Amma gives the example of rowing a boat without untying it from the shore; we are never going reach the other shore that way. Moreover, we should not disobey the advice of our Guru (as Sati disobeyed Shiva by attending the yagna), though at times it may be against our wishes. Daksha represents the ego, which expects to receive respect from everyone including Realized Masters. When that expectation is not fulfilled, anger and envy follow. Daksha's death symbolizes the destruction of the ego, while his new head symbolizes a spiritual rebirth. Once the ego is gone, all hostilities vanish and every word that comes out of us is a prayer.

Arjuna's war became a yagna or offering to God — all because of the attitude of the one performing the action.

Many of us worship Amma and serve Amma, but we do not always have the right attitude in our worship or in our service. I remember a humorous incident. Once when Amma was giving darshan, it was so hot that one devotee asked Amma's permission to fan Her. Amma agreed, and this devotee was fanning Amma for some time when another devotee came and asked the first devotee for a chance to fan Amma as well. The first devotee replied adamantly, "No, Amma gave permission only for me to do it; I am not going to give you a turn." The second devotee waited for some time, but the first devotee never yielded. Finally, the second devotee took another fan and also started to fan Amma. The first devotee who was fanning Amma wanted to give more air to Amma than the second devotee was giving, so she started to fan more vigorously, and then a competition arose. Each one tried to outdo the other in fanning Amma.

Finally, Amma felt suffocated. She said, "Stop, stop. I don't want anyone to fan me." Here they had been doing personal service to Amma, yet their attitude had been one of competition. Because of their attitude, their service became a nuisance to Amma.

Anyone who spends time with Amma will get a chance to do some sort of personal service for Her, such as handing Amma the prasad which She gives to the devotees or helping with the darshan line. (There are also limitless opportunities for service through participating in the ashram's spiritual and humanitarian activities.) Amma creates these opportunities in order to give us a chance to be close to Her and to help us become fit to receive Her grace. We are incredibly fortunate to have such opportunities but most of the time, because of our negativities, we do not receive the full benefit these chances afford us.

Amma tells a story in this regard. There were two disciples and a Guru. These two disciples were always very competitive about their service to their Guru. If the Guru asked one disciple to do something, the other disciple would get jealous and pick a quarrel or otherwise abuse the disciple who had gotten the chance to serve the Guru. The Guru often advised them to rid themselves of their feelings of competition and jealousy, but they did not heed his words. Finally, the Guru decided, "Whatever work I ask them to do, I am going to divide it between them. I will ask each one to do half of the work so there won't be any competition or hatred between them. If I ask one to bring me something to drink once, the second time I am going to ask the other."

One day, the Guru's legs were aching. He decided to call one of his disciples to give him a massage. Then he immediately thought, "Oh, no, if I call one disciple, the other disciple is going to get angry with him. I better call both of them." So the Guru called both disciples and asked one to massage his right leg, and the other to massage his left.

The disciples were very happy as they were each massaging one of his legs. Then the Guru fell asleep, and in his sleep, he wanted to turn onto one side. He was lying flat on his back and wanted to turn onto his right side, so naturally he lifted his left leg and put it over his right. The disciple who was massaging his right leg looked up and said to the other disciple, "This is my territory. The leg you are massaging should not come here." He thought the other disciple was putting the Guru's leg there.

The other disciple didn't say anything because he knew it was the Guru who had moved his leg. He went on massaging the

Guru's left leg even though it was encroaching on the first disciple's territory. Then the first disciple snapped, "I told you not to put your leg here. This is my side. Take it away from here." Saying so, he pushed the left leg back to the left side. The other disciple said, "How can you do that? This is the Guru's leg." Saying thus, he pushed it back to the right side. They went on pushing the Guru's leg back and forth, and then finally the first disciple lost his temper. Taking a big stick, he gave the left leg a good beating.

In this situation who is really suffering? The disciples were doing personal service to the Guru, but because of their jealousy and possessiveness, the Guru had to suffer. This is what happened with Amma as well when the two devotees were competing with each other to fan Her.

The Guru is always showering grace upon us, but we must become a fit vessel for that grace in order to receive it. With the right attitude, almost any action can bring us closer to God, while even the most righteous action performed with the wrong attitude can block God's grace from reaching us.

For example, the scriptures say it is not wrong to tell a lie if your motivation is to spare someone's feelings. During the 2004 South Indian Tour, Amma visited Rameshwaram in Tamil Nadu at the southernmost tip of India. A group of young men came for Amma's darshan together. The leader of the group said loudly, "Amma! Do you remember me?" Before Amma could answer, he continued, "Amma, I was your classmate in the 8th standard!" All of us standing near Amma were certain he was not telling the truth. This man seemed at least 20 years younger than Amma. He turned to his friends and added, "Amma and I were classmates at the town high school." We all expected Amma to correct him. Instead, Amma affirmed his claim, saying, "Yes, yes!" and embraced him lovingly.

Afterward, we wanted to ask Amma about Her strange response, but the crowd was so big that we did not get a chance. Later, Amma explained, "Amma never went to that boy's town high school. Amma has studied only at the school in Kuzhitura (a village near the ashram), and She has studied only up to the 4th standard.[9] Still, Amma did not want to tell the boy he was wrong. He probably wanted to show his friends that he had been very familiar with Amma since his childhood. Had Amma admonished him before his friends, it would have caused a very deep scar in his heart. Instead of carrying a heavy heart, Amma wanted him to carry sweet memories of his darshan."

As always, Amma's action in this case was in perfect accordance with the scriptures. There is a saying in the Vedas, "*Satyam bruyat, priyam bruyat, na bruyat satyamapriyam.*" This means, "Speak the truth; speak only pleasing words; do not speak unkind words even if they are true."

Thus, we cannot say that telling the truth is always a good action and telling a lie is always a bad action. If our intention is to hurt someone by telling the truth, it becomes a bad action. If our intention is to protect someone by telling a lie, it becomes a good action.

Everything — whether we create good prarabdha or bad prarabdha, whether an action helps or hinders our efforts to become fit to receive God's grace — depends on our attitude or intention. ❖

---

[9] Amma left school at the age of nine in order to care for the needs of Her family, as Her mother had fallen ill.

CHAPTER 13

Selfishness & Selflessness

A selfless attitude always brings Amma closer to us. Every Tuesday at Amritapuri the residents of the ashram spend the morning in meditation and Amma comes to the prayer hall to serve us lunch. There is usually quite a big crowd; Amma serves well over 2,000 plates. While receiving Amma's prasad, one devotee accidentally dropped the plate at Her feet. The plate was overturned, spilling the curry and rice on the floor.

As there were still quite a few people waiting to receive food from Amma, I started to clean up the mess so people would not step in it. However, as I was cleaning up the food with my bare hands, it occurred to me that if my hands got dirty, I would have to wash them before eating Amma's prasad. And if I left to go wash my hands, I thought Amma might ask someone to sit there, and I would lose my spot. Thinking thus, I stopped cleaning up the spill.

Meanwhile, another brahmachari knelt down and wiped the floor clean, also with his bare hands. After he cleaned up the mess, even though his hands were dirty, he didn't leave to wash his hands. He just stood near Amma and watched Her continue to serve prasad. When his turn came to receive prasad, he took the plate and then turned to leave. Amma stopped him and asked him to sit near Her. Then Amma asked everyone to eat. Just as this brahmachari was about to begin eating, Amma caught hold of his hand, saying, "My son, your hands are dirty." She took a pitcher of water and washed his hands. She also fed him a few morsels of food with Her own hands.

When I saw this, I knew I had made a mistake. I had been thinking only about myself, whereas the other brahmachari had thought only about serving Amma and the devotees by cleaning up the mess. Even though I had started doing service by cleaning the floor, my selfishness was stronger than my attitude of service. I had been motivated by a desire to remain close to Amma, but by not giving a second thought to himself, the other brahmachari had been able to come even closer to Amma. When these thoughts dawned in my mind, Amma looked at me and smiled mischievously.

We get many such opportunities to earn Amma's grace. Unfortunately, most of the time, due to our selfishness and ego, we throw these opportunities away.

Once a man fell into a deep ditch and could not get out. After a long time, a passerby happened to hear his groans and peered over the edge of the ditch. "Help!" the man in the ditch exclaimed. "I've fallen into this ditch and I can't get out!"

The passerby simply shrugged, "It's your prarabdha—you must face the consequences of your past actions," and continued on his way.

After some more time had passed, another person happened upon the man in the ditch. "What happened to you?" the passerby asked.

"I was walking along and I fell into the ditch," the man groaned.

"Didn't you see the warning sign posted here on the roadside? You should be more careful in the future!" he advised and kept walking. A little later, a third person walked by the ditch and, hearing the groans, peered over the edge. The third person didn't even ask what happened. He just climbed down into the ditch, lifted the fallen man on his shoulder and carried him out.

These three passersby illustrate the three ways we can respond toward the suffering of others. When we see someone suffering, we can simply say that it is their prarabdha and let them deal with it. Alternatively, we can offer them advice and point out their mistakes. Finally, we can accept their suffering as our own, doing whatever it takes to uplift them. Most of us will respond in one of the first two ways. The third way is Amma's way. Let us all aspire to develop a heart overflowing with compassion so that we can also see the suffering of others as our own. This attitude will benefit us spiritually and can even transform society and the world.

Amma says, "One who has love for God will surely have compassion for those who suffer. Devotion and selfless service are not two but one; they are two faces of the same coin."

Once I had taken the ashram bus (at that time there was only one) to a workshop to get it repaired just before we were scheduled to depart on a tour of Kerala. Unexpectedly, the repair took more than a full day and I had to stay overnight. I lay down in the bus but I was unable to sleep as the repair work went on throughout the night. Finally, on the evening of the second day, I drove back to the ashram. When I arrived, I saw that Amma and the brahmacharis had already crossed the river and were waiting for the bus, for we had planned to leave that afternoon.

As I had not eaten, slept or had a bath since leaving the ashram the morning of the previous day, I must have looked weary and worn-out. Amma approached me and asked me what had caused the delay. I explained what had happened, and then I went to start the bus so we could leave immediately. Amma called me back and moved forward to embrace me. I told Amma, "Please don't touch me, Amma. I haven't taken a bath, and I am stinking with sweat." Amma didn't listen to my protests. Wrapping Her arms around me, She said, "The sweat of selfless service is like perfume for me." She then asked another brahmachari to drive the bus and made me sit next to Her until we stopped for dinner.

Amma doesn't want anything from anyone for the kindness and love She offers others, but She would be happy if we would do our part to help others. We can do this by working selflessly to alleviate the suffering of the poor and needy. The present day world needs such sincere and selfless people. Otherwise, there will only be more suffering and problems. In this context, I remember the statement of the former Prime Minister of India, Atal Behari Vajpayee, during the inauguration of Amma's super-specialty hospital (AIMS). He said, "The world today needs proof that our human values are useful, that such qualities as compassion, selflessness, renunciation, and humility have the power to create a great and prosperous society. Amma's work provides us with the much-needed proof."

Amma does not expect us to do something that we are unable to do. She does not expect a fish to haul a massive load the way a mule can. Nor does She expect a mule to swim in the sea. Amma only expects us to live as compassionate, loving, and caring human beings. ❖

CHAPTER 14

Satsang: The First Step in Spiritual Life

The first step in spiritual life is *satsang*. *Sat* means the Supreme Truth. *Sang* means association. Therefore, in the real sense of the term, satsang means to associate with the Truth or be in communion with the Truth. However, since most of us are not able to do that, the best form of satsang is to be in association with one who abides in the Truth. If it is not possible for us to spend time in the company of a Realized Master, we should, at least, try to associate with people who are spiritually minded. In their presence, we will be able to think of God and remember the goal of human life. That is why Amma asks all Her devotees to gather together at regular intervals to sing God's praise, chant, meditate, pray, read spiritual books, and have spiritual discussions. This is also called satsang.

Whenever we participate in any form of satsang with sincerity and concentration, we are able to create positive vibrations within ourselves. There are so many attractions and distractions in the world. When we indulge in many of the present-day pastimes, we invite a lot of unnecessary turbulence into our mind — we become agitated and tense. Satsang helps us keep our mind above all these attractions and distractions. This will help us to remain relatively calm and peaceful.

There is a folk story about the painter Leonardo da Vinci, whose most famous painting is that of the Last Supper. The story goes that when da Vinci decided to portray the Last Supper, he sent people far and wide with the hope of finding a person whose overall countenance would be representative of Jesus, as he wanted to paint Jesus first.

Da Vinci's representatives brought back the perfect fit — a handsome, upright young man with good manners. Da Vinci used the young man as a model for Jesus, and was very happy with the result. He then went on to portray each of the disciples, modeled after 11 other men who were brought to him. By this time, several years had passed since he began the painting, and only one disciple was yet to be depicted. That was Judas, the disciple who betrayed Jesus for just 30 pieces of silver.

Once again, the great artist sent out a search party. This time, their assignment was to find a man whose cruel looks and wicked demeanor would be suitable for the portrayal of Judas. Finally, they brought back a man whose appearance was testimony to many years of anger, hatred, and selfishness. Da Vinci was satisfied and began to paint the final disciple. It was then that the man he had chosen to model Judas began to sob uncontrollably. Da Vinci stopped painting and asked the man why he was crying.

The man looked at da Vinci and said, "Can you not recognize me?"

Da Vinci looked closer but could not place the man's face. "I'm sure I've never seen you before," he said apologetically.

"Look at your own painting," the man pleaded with the artist. "I am the very same man you chose to portray Jesus so many years ago."

Da Vinci looked closely and saw that it was true. Due to years of spending time in bad company and performing selfish and hurtful actions, the same man who had so well represented Jesus was now a perfect match for the man who had betrayed him.

Depending on the company we keep or the associations we have, we will naturally develop the corresponding qualities. That is why Amma places so much importance on satsang. Amma gives the following example: In India you will find certain temples where the parrots chant divine names such as "Ram, Ram, Ram, Ram," or "Hare, Hare, Hare, Hare," or a mantra such as "Om Namah Shivaya." A parrot living near the temple will be able to chant these divine names and mantras because it hears the devotees chanting the same while they are visiting the temple. At the same time, if a parrot happens to live near a liquor shop or a bar where people drink and abuse each other with vulgar words, the parrot will pick up only those words.

People have varying degrees of spiritual inclination. When a person with even a minimal interest in spirituality participates in any form of satsang, that spark of interest can be kindled.

Amma says bad habits are like wild fire — they spread very quickly — while good habits take a long time to make an impression. If we indulge in something three or four times, we will be totally enslaved by it. For example, if we drink coffee four days in a row, on the fifth day we will have a headache if we don't drink coffee. But when it comes to good habits, such as keeping a regular timetable for spiritual practice or always speaking kind words, even if we are told about their importance a hundred times, we are not serious about putting them into practice. We will certainly not get a headache if we don't!

Our desires and attachments will always pull our mind down into worldly affairs. Thus, our mind needs something to lift it upward. Amma often gives the following example:

When scientists launch a rocket into space, the first stage rocket will take the satellite only to an orbit around earth. To overcome the force of the earth's gravity, a booster rocket is needed. Similarly, our mind is trapped in an orbit around the ego. If we want to break free, we too need a booster rocket — a Spiritual Master. The Master will pull us away from the attractive force of the ego and take us straight to God. With all obstacles from our path removed, we will be able to transcend all limitations and attain true freedom.

Many of us were not at all interested in spirituality before coming to Amma. After seeing Amma, we became interested in spiritual practice and a spiritual life. However, if something unfortunate happens in our life, our interest in spirituality can drop off as suddenly as it appeared. We may also forget all about spirituality when things are going extremely well, thinking that we no longer need God's help. At that time, we need to be reminded that it is only due to God's grace that we are doing so well. Thus, we need satsang both to kindle our interest in spirituality and to sustain it over the long term.

Amma gives the following example: If we throw a piece of iron into water, it will sink. But if we mount that same piece of iron on a buoyant material, such as a block of wood, it will float. Likewise, satsang can help prevent our mind from becoming totally immersed in the attractions and distractions of the world (we may get wet, but we won't drown). This becomes much easier if we have a Satguru. Through the Satguru's unconditional love and compassion and by observing his or her example, we are able to overcome many of our selfish desires and attachments. Those of us who are with Amma can understand this statement from our own personal experience. There are countless examples of people who have renounced their attractions to various objects of the world after meeting Amma. Instead of pursuing worldly achievements and acquisitions, they now spend their free time performing spiritual practice and in serving others.

The Great Master Adi Shankaracharya said,

satsangatve nissangatvam
nissangatve nirmohatvam
nirmohatve niscala tatvam
niscalatatve jīvan muktiḥ

Through satsang we will be able to overcome our attachments. By overcoming our attachments, we overcome the delusion that objects of the world can give us lasting happiness. When we overcome this delusion, the mind becomes calm and still. This stillness of mind leads to freedom from bondage while still alive in this body.

During satsang, apart from praying and meditating, we discuss spiritual topics and principles. This helps us to understand the nature of the world and its objects. We start to analyze the world rationally; we realize that we are attached to so many people and things in the world, and each time one of these people or objects changes or leaves us, we experience sorrow. When we begin to understand that God is eternal and everything else will disappear one day, we are able to develop an attitude of detachment toward everything save God, or the Atman.

Through detachment, we are able to overcome delusion. Here, delusion refers to the misconception that "I cannot be happy without having a certain object, person, achievement, etc." If we are detached from these things, we will stop pursuing them, thus overcoming this delusion. For example, a heavy smoker goes to see Amma for the first time. He receives darshan and then sits next to Amma for a long time. By the time he leaves Amma's side, he realizes three hours have passed. Normally, he would have smoked at least six cigarettes during that time, and he would have been very agitated if he had not gotten a chance to smoke. However, the thought of smoking a cigarette did not even occur to him once when he was sitting near Amma, and he was actually much happier than usual. Thus, he realizes that his belief that he needs cigarettes to be happy is a misconception. Through satsang with Amma, he was able to become detached from smoking, which allowed him to overcome the delusion that he needed cigarettes in order to be happy.

Before coming to the ashram, the life ambition of one of the brahmacharis was to become a movie star. He felt that if he could not become a famous actor, his life would be wasted. He actually came to Amma to seek Her blessings to achieve his goal. When he met Amma, he was overwhelmed by Her love and stayed at the ashram for a few days. When he returned home, he found that his desire to be near Amma was so great that he came back to the ashram and never went home again. His desire to become a movie star completely fell away. Through his love for Amma, he became detached from the world, and he was able to overcome his deluded notion of happiness and fulfillment.

When these delusions disappear, our mind becomes relatively still and peaceful. When we are deluded, thinking a certain object will give us happiness, we will strive to attain that object. Whether we get it or not, our mind becomes agitated by the struggle. When we are free of this delusion, our mind is at rest; it is calm and quiet.

With such a still and peaceful mind, we are able to gain one-pointed concentration in our spiritual practices, which will ultimately lead us to *jivanmukti* (liberation while still living in the body). In that state, we are not influenced by anything. Without the aid of any outside object or person, we feel totally happy and content — we have achieved the ultimate success.

Amma gives another example about a parrot. Suppose we train a parrot to say mantras. It will say them, but what if we let it out of the cage and a cat catches it? The parrot will not say mantras at that moment! Instead, it will scream in its own way. This is because the mantras have not gone deep into its heart. Similarly, satsang must be embraced with an open heart for us to receive the desired benefit. Amma always says that just as a person visiting a perfume factory comes out with a fragrant air — though he or she may not have bought or applied any scent — no one returns from the company of a Mahatma without benefiting at least a little. However, if we are receptive and free of preconceived notions, we can benefit so much more. The seeds of grace cannot sprout on the rocks of the ego, but in the fertile soil of a childlike heart, they will grow and produce a bountiful harvest.

As a spiritual seeker, try to participate in some form of satsang as often as you can. ❀

CHAPTER 15

A Pilgrimage or a Picnic

In India, many people undertake a pilgrimage at some point in their lives. In a sense, going on a pilgrimage can also be considered a satsang, for when we go on a pilgrimage to a holy place, it helps us to keep our mind focused on the spiritual goal.

A pilgrimage is actually very simple; it means traveling to a temple or a holy place and coming back. Nowadays, however, the pilgrims will come across many attractions while traveling. They will pass by good restaurants, nice hotels, movies, shopping malls, even a circus or a magic show. If the pilgrims are not careful, they will be diverted by these things and even forget the real purpose of their journey — ending up on a holiday picnic instead of a pilgrimage.

One of Amma's devotees told me a story. He had a friend who had gone on a pilgrimage to a renowned Shiva temple in North India, and this devotee happened to visit him afterward. When the devotee went to his friend's house, he saw a life-size picture of his host sitting on a camel. The devotee asked his friend, "What is this? Where did you ride on a camel?"

"When I visited that Shiva temple," his friend answered.

The devotee asked him, "Did you have to go on a pilgrimage to ride on a camel? You could have done that in the next village."

His aim had been to go and pay his respects to Lord Shiva and come back. Instead of buying a picture of Lord Shiva, the man bought a very big picture of himself riding on a camel.

See how the mind gets distracted? The entrepreneurs understand the nature of the mind, insofar as they know that even people who go on a pilgrimage are not wholly focused on God. Thus we can see people making money in all sorts of ways — from elephant, horse and camel rides to fancy restaurants, five-star hotels, pizza parlors, and even video arcades — at India's most sacred pilgrimage sites and places of worship.

Naturally, we will be attracted to these opportunities. "Oh!" we will think, "I never rode on a camel before, so let me take this chance." Even if we go on a pilgrimage, we are not able to concentrate on the purpose of our trip.

Many years ago, in order to fulfill the desires of some of the brahmacharis, Amma took us on a pilgrimage to Tiruvannamalai, a holy place in Tamil Nadu. This was the site of Sri Ramana Maharshi's ashram and the sacred mountain, Arunachala. We stayed there for two days. On the first day, as usual we woke up before dawn and performed our morning prayers and meditation. Amma took us to visit the temple and to the top of the mountain. When we returned to the house, She went to Her room, leaving us to our own devices, as we were tired from the journey up the mountain. After having a good meal, we spent the afternoon chatting and resting without doing any spiritual practices. That night, after the evening bhajans, Amma asked us how we had spent our time that day. As we had not done anything worthwhile, we couldn't give a satisfactory answer. After hearing our reply, Amma went to Her room without uttering another word.

The next morning, we again got up at the usual time. Normally, the first thing we would do upon waking is to take a bath — according to tradition, one should take a bath before beginning one's morning prayers. However, because of laziness, a few of us were reluctant to have a bath. Though it was actually not very cold outside, we told ourselves it was too cold for a bath.

Just then, we heard someone shouting that Amma had come out. We looked outside and saw Amma walking toward the road to Mount Arunachala with Swami Paramatmananda at Her side. He looked back at us and told us Amma was going to circumambulate the mountain. Even though some of us had been feeling lazy moments before, when we found out Amma was already on Her way, we quickly took a cold shower and ran after Her.

On Her way around the mountain, Amma stopped before every shrine and cave and asked us to chant "Om," three times. In some places, She also asked us to sit and meditate. It usually takes about an hour and a half to walk around the mountain, but it took us six hours. We spent the rest of the day in meditation and singing bhajans. Later Amma told us that if She had not come out that morning, we would have wasted the second day of our pilgrimage as well. By Her example, Amma was showing us the proper way to conduct ourselves on a pilgrimage.

We should be very careful and alert even in seemingly simple practices like making a pilgrimage. Even a small amount of carelessness can defeat the purpose. What to say, then, about more subtle practices like meditation? We have to be very vigilant. For a spiritual seeker, it's better to stay away from distractions and diversions whenever we can.

In Kerala, there is a famous temple called Sabarimala situated in the middle of a forest. The forest is home to many wild animals such as tigers, elephants, and bears. Until about 30 years ago, it was a very dangerous trek. Now they have made a road through the forest, and the journey is much less dangerous.

The temple is dedicated to Lord Ayyappa. As a part of the tradition of this temple, devotees intending to make the pilgrimage to Sabarimala should observe strict vows for 41 days before making the journey. During this time, they observe celibacy as well as abstain from smoking, drinking, and eating meat. In earlier days, they would make the pilgrimage on foot. The pilgrims would cook their food and even sleep on the roadside. They were at the mercy of nature. If it were raining, they would get drenched in the rain; if it were a hot day, they would get baked in the sun. They would also carry on their head a bundle of coconuts, ghee and rice to offer to God while worshipping at the temple. If they didn't have this bundle, or *irumudi*, they wouldn't be let inside the temple. All this *tapas* (austerities) was their way of expressing their devotion to God. By the time they had come back, they would have earned some spiritual energy by giving up all their comforts and following such a strict discipline.

Nowadays, most people are not strictly following all these disciplines. Many people no longer observe the 41 days of vows. Rather than making the pilgrimage on foot, most people take the bus. If you don't have the irumudi, they will not allow you to climb the 18 sacred steps to the main entrance of the temple, but it is possible to enter through the side or rear entrance. Many people now prefer to take all these shortcuts. In doing so, however, much of the purpose of the pilgrimage has been lost. Along with the destination, the effort we put forth and the observances we follow along the way are very important. These are what give us spiritual strength and help us to earn God's grace. We cannot simply drive to Sabarimala and walk in through the back door, hoping to receive the same benefit as those who have sincerely undertaken the pilgrimage.

Amma tells the following joke. There was a boy who came home from school one day with a big smile. The father asked his son, "What happened at school today? Why are you so happy?" The boy replied, "Today, there was an athletic competition in our school. I finished the 400-meter race in 20 seconds."

"What? Even the world record is more than twice that. How could you possibly run 400 meters in only 20 seconds?"

"I took a shortcut," the boy said.

If the boy took a shortcut, how could it be called a 400-meter race? Likewise, if we don't follow the required disciplines, the very spirit of the pilgrimage is defeated. The purpose of a pilgrimage is to gain God's grace, but even for that we want to take a shortcut. In truth, there is no shortcut to receive God's grace.

Once, a devotee had a vision of God. When he saw God, he thanked Him for appearing and sang his praises. God remained before Him for a long time. The devotee was able to clear up all his doubts and matters of faith. Still, God didn't go anywhere. So the devotee thought he would ask something about God's realm. He asked, "Oh Lord, what is time like in Heaven?"

God smiled and replied, "One million years on Earth is equal to just one minute in heaven."

The devotee was astonished and ventured a further question. "Oh Lord, what is the value of currency of heaven?"

"One dollar in My realm is worth one million dollars on Earth," God told the devotee.

The devotee could not believe his ears. He had one more question for God. "Oh merciful Lord, if it is so, would you please give me one heavenly dollar?"

"Sure," the Lord replied. "Just wait a minute."

Amma always says that God's grace can only be gained through putting forth sincere effort. For many people, a trip to Amma's ashram is a long journey of planes, trains, and automobiles, and life at the ashram may not be as comfortable as the life they are accustomed to at home.

Nowadays, one can find all the basic necessities at the ashram and can even check email. In the early days of the ashram, the situation was very different. We often had no electricity. There was no running water; we had to carry water from the village tap. Sometimes even the village tap would not have any water for several days, and we would have to go to the village across the river just to get drinking water. At first, there was not even any place to sleep. Because Amma's sisters were living in the family house, Amma's parents did not want the brahmacharis coming into the house at night. We would sleep outside on the sand. If it were raining at night, we would just sit inside the temple. Seeing our plight Amma also refused to sleep inside the house. Many nights She wouldn't sleep at all. Other times She would sleep outside, lying down in front of the house some distance away from the brahmacharis.

Later, when Swami Paramatmananda (then Br. Nealu) came to stay at the ashram, he had enough money with him to build a small hut. Inside the hut, there was a kitchen, a storeroom and just enough room for four or five of us to sleep inside. Even though we had a kitchen at that point, most of the time there were not enough groceries to prepare food. Sometimes Amma's devotees brought food for us, but if more devotees came then Amma would use the food to feed them instead. Amma always insisted the devotees got something to eat when they came to the ashram, even if it meant She and the brahmacharis had to go without food. At times such as this, Amma would sometimes go to the neighboring houses and receive *bhiksha* (food offerings) for us.

Even though it was a hard life by any standard, we never felt as though we were suffering. We were so focused on Amma that we did not miss any of the usual comforts of the world, even the basic necessities like food, water, and a roof over our heads.

Later, even when we had the means, Amma agreed only to provide the minimum comforts in the ashram. She wanted to inculcate a spirit of renunciation in everyone who came to the ashram. Amma said, "When people come to the ashram, they are renouncing at least some of their comforts. In this way they will gain some spiritual benefit." Amma is very particular that when you come to Her ashram — spending so much time, money, and energy — you must gain some spiritual strength, some spiritual benefit to take home with you. That is why even today, when people from all over the world come to the ashram, it is not like a resort. You will have to make some kind of sacrifice to stay there.

So for Amma's children, coming to Amritapuri can be a great pilgrimage. But when we come, we should remember to try to complete the pilgrimage in the right spirit. If we have to put up with any discomfort or make a small sacrifice, let us see it as a way to develop spiritual strength and become fit to receive Amma's divine grace. ❖

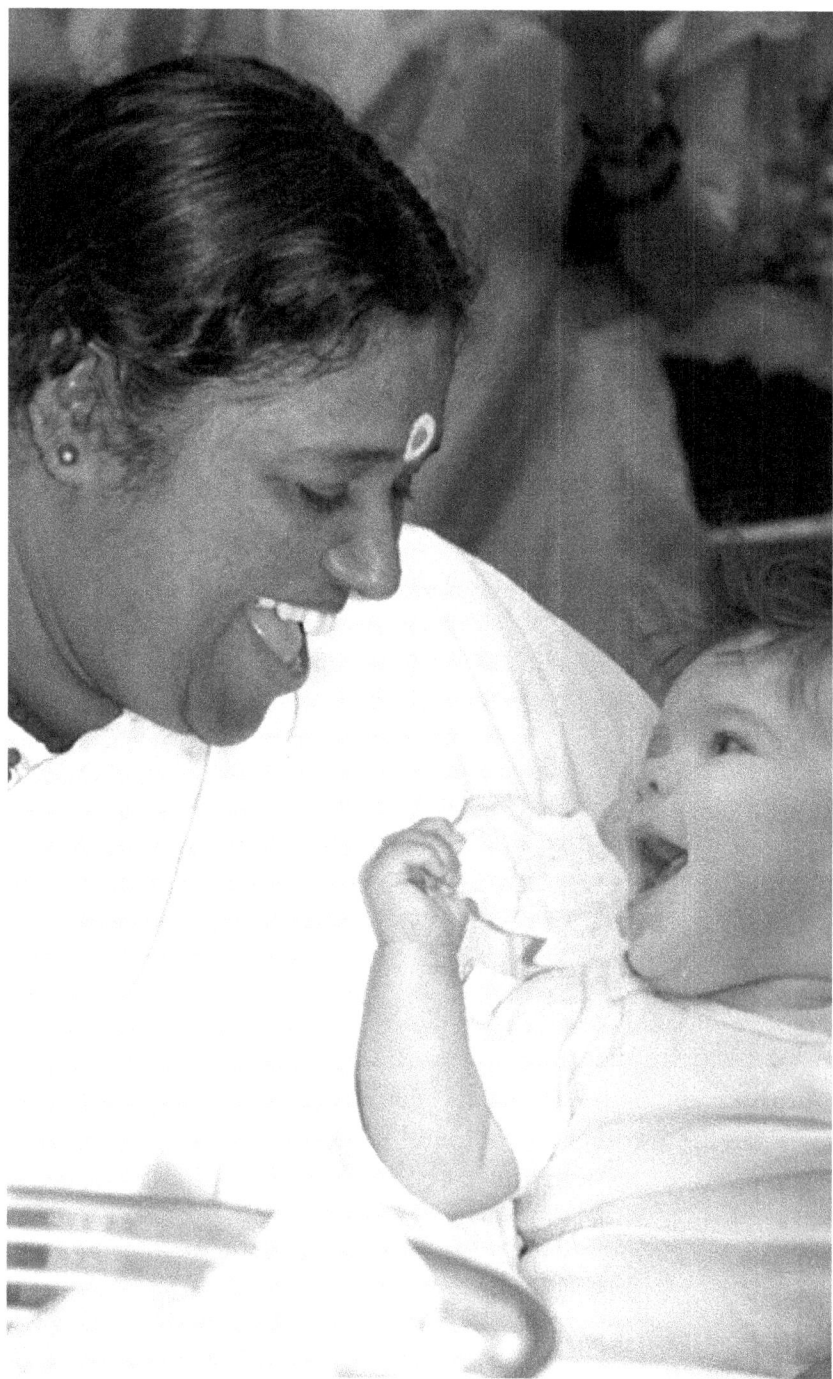

CHAPTER 16

The Unique Power of Discrimination

Certain things are common for human beings and all other living beings. These include food, sleep, procreation, and the need for security. But human beings have one quality that sets them apart from all other beings. This quality is not intelligence; animals do have intelligence to some extent. What makes human beings unique is the power of discrimination.[10] For an ordinary person, discrimination means the ability to distinguish between right and wrong, and between what is beneficial and what is harmful. For a spiritual seeker, discrimination means all that and more. A spiritual seeker should be able to use his or her discrimination to distinguish between that which is permanent — God, or Truth — and that which is changing or impermanent.

The very intelligence that has helped human beings create prosperity has also been the cause of our misery and suffering. This is because we are not using our power of discrimination properly. Intelligence without discrimination can lead to destruction. When humans commit rape, murder, acts of oppression,

---

[10] The Latin origins of the word "discriminate" are *discriminare* (to divide) and *discernere* (to separate). In the West, discrimination is usually associated with some form of prejudice. However, according to Vedanta, real discrimination is the power of separating the changeless and eternal Self from the changing and perishable world.

or terrorist attacks, or when they create circumstances that lead to poverty and hunger for others, it is because they are not using their discrimination. If people used the very same faculties of the body, mind, and intellect to serve others, to wipe away their tears and alleviate their suffering, the world could be transformed into heaven. For this, we need discrimination.

When we use our discrimination along with our intelligence, we will use our human capacities to promote harmony and goodwill among all. This means performing loving, compassionate and selfless actions. This not only helps the world but also the individuals performing the actions. When we use our discrimination to perform good actions, our mind becomes pure and expansive.

Amma says that even though human beings have achieved so much power, there are many things that are not under our control. For example, we cannot decide where we should be born, or who our parents should be, or what talents or capacities we should have. If we could make these decisions for ourselves, this world would be a very different place. Because we have no say in these circumstances, we are each born with different talents and capacities but also with a number of weaknesses and defects. Under these circumstances, in order to succeed in life, we have to focus on our strengths while recognizing our weaknesses. Unfortunately, many people do the opposite.

Instead of concentrating on their strengths and talents, they concentrate on their weaknesses without recognizing their strengths. Thus, many people leave the world with wonderful treasures still hidden within them. Psychologists say that human beings use only 10-12 percent of their potential. It is said that even Einstein used only 25 percent of his intellectual capacity. If that is true, it means that we all have a great deal of untapped potential within us. Using our capacity of discrimination, we can utilize more of our inner potential by transforming our weaknesses into strengths.

A woman in the United States lost her son because of a drunk driver. She could easily have been consumed by hatred for the man who killed her son. Instead of fighting with the drunk driver, she chose to fight drunk driving. In 1980 she and a group of women in California founded MADD (Mothers Against Drunk Driving). The organization now has 600 chapters nationwide; their activism paved the way for legislation against drunk driving, and the percentage of drunk drivers in the United States has been dramatically reduced as a result. What could this woman have accomplished by just getting angry with one individual? Instead, by using her discrimination, she was able to channel her anger into something that really benefited society.

A similar case occurred in a rural village of tribal people in India. Since they were very poor, many of them did not have proper houses. Some houses did not even have doors. One night, a vagabond entered one of the houses and tried to rape a woman who was sleeping inside. She was able to fight him off, but she was badly injured while defending herself. While recovering from her injuries, the victim was burning with anger. However, instead of trying to take revenge on that individual, she used her anger in a creative way. Resolving that no one else should have to suffer the same fate, she organized the members of the tribe to protest their living conditions before the local government. Finally, the government agreed to build proper, secure homes for the whole tribe. They also created a special police force to guard that area.

In the address Amma delivered at the Global Peace Initiative of Women Religious and Spiritual Leaders (2002), She tells a true story about a woman whose husband was killed in a terrorist attack. Her son was a young boy at the time, and when he lost his father, he vowed that one day he would take revenge. He planned to join a rival group of militants to retaliate against the group that killed his father. When he told his mother of his plan, she advised him, "Son, look at the painful state of our family. Look how difficult it is to make both ends meet without your father. And just look at yourself, how sad you are, not knowing the love of a father as you are growing up. When you see other fathers taking their children to school, don't you feel sad, wishing you had a father? By taking revenge on those who killed your father, what else will you accomplish but to create more suffering and sorrow? Should there be any more sorrowful faces in society? What we should really strive for is to develop love and kinship. That is the only way to gain peace both for us and for others. Therefore, my son, discriminate and act as you feel is most appropriate." The boy took his mother's words to heart and refused to join any terrorist group even when they tried to recruit him. Years later, when he met Amma, he offered Her a prayer — "Please give those terrorists, who are so full of hatred and violence, the right understanding. And for all those who have faced so many atrocities and have suffered so much, please fill their hearts with the spirit of forgiveness. Otherwise, the situation will only deteriorate, and there will be no end to the violence."

Amma points out that the anti-venom that saves lives is actually extracted from the very same poison we get from the snakebite. In the same way, by acting with discrimination and good intentions, our negative emotions and weaknesses can be transformed into strengths.

On the other hand, if we do not act with discrimination, even our strengths or talents can become weaknesses. For example, we see many people whose speaking talents allow them to excel in sales. However, when they talk too much to a customer, instead of persuading the customer to buy the product, they can drive them away. Their strength of speaking can be used to sell the product. But if they go on speaking, they may talk the customer right out of the sale. Thus, their speaking ability becomes a weakness.

I have heard a joke that illustrates this point. During the French Revolution, three men were escorted to the guillotine. A priest accompanied them in order to administer the Last Rites. The first man was instructed to place his head on the chopping block. When the blade was released, it did not fall on his neck but remained stuck where it was. The priest took it as a sign from God and released the man, saying that God had forgiven his mistakes. The same thing happened to the second man. The third man happened to be an engineer by profession. As he was being taken to the guillotine, he looked up and exclaimed, "Hey, I see the problem!" and gave instructions for repairing the guillotine. The guillotine was promptly fixed, and the engineer lost his head. Here the engineer was using his talents without using his discrimination.

It is necessary to use our discrimination when we are choosing the values we wish to live by. If we do not, even the best objects and opportunities in life will become useless and bring us misery. Many of you will have heard the phrase "Midas touch," which means the ability to make large amounts of money with very little apparent effort. This expression comes from the Greek myth of King Midas, whose greatest ambition was to accumulate wealth. One day a goddess appeared before him and offered him a boon; he could ask for whatever he liked. The king was overjoyed. He asked the goddess to bless him so that whatever he touched would turn into gold. The goddess warned him about the consequences of this boon, but his greed was so great that he did not heed her words. He would accept no other boon. Finally, the goddess blessed him with the boon he requested. From that moment onward, whatever the king touched turned to gold.

It was not long before the king began to encounter serious difficulties. When he sat down to his breakfast, all the food he touched was transformed into gold. As he could not eat a bowl of golden cereal, he called his only daughter to help him. She came running to his room and he lovingly hugged her. Lo, she immediately became a golden statue. The king was shocked and distressed. He started crying loudly and prayed to the goddess who had given him the boon. The goddess appeared before him and asked the king whether he was happy with his golden touch. The king pleaded with the goddess to bring his daughter back to life and to please take back his golden touch.

This story shows that distorted values lead to tragedy. Sometimes not getting what we want is a bigger boon than having our desire fulfilled. Discrimination can help us to cultivate positive values. This, in turn, will make our life both peaceful and useful for us and for others.

I heard a beautiful story from a devotee of Amma. Before meeting Amma, she used to spend time at another ashram. She arrived at that ashram very late one night, and when she got to her assigned dormitory room, she turned on the light so she could find her way to her bed. The moment the room was illuminated, the woman heard an angry voice from across the room say, "Turn off the light!"

The woman shyly turned out the light and felt her way along the wall to her bed, making up her bed in the dark. Shortly after she had crawled into bed, another newcomer arrived and turned on the light as she entered. Again, the angry voice exclaimed, "Turn off the light!" During the brief time the room had been lit up, the first woman saw that the newcomer was Japanese and that she was wearing an orange dot indicating that it was her first time visiting the ashram.

Even though the first woman was very tired, she thought that the newcomer must be even more exhausted and disoriented. She rose from her bed and went to greet the newcomer. Bowing in the traditional Japanese style, she took the newcomer's sheets from her hand and proceeded to make up her bed for her.

Then she bowed again to the grateful new arrival and returned to her bed. Before she fell asleep, the door to the dormitory opened once again, and once again, the light was switched on. Like clockwork, again came the command, "Turn off the light!" The first woman was preparing to rise from her bed again when she saw the Japanese woman get out of her bed and greet the third arrival of the night. The Japanese woman bowed to the third person, took her sheets, and made up her bed for her. The Japanese woman simply assumed that this was the custom at that ashram.

This story shows us that we learn by example, but we can use our discrimination to choose which examples to follow and which to disregard. The Japanese woman could have easily decided to join in the command to turn off the light. Instead, she wisely and discriminately chose to follow the more selfless example of the woman who had offered a helping hand.

I recall another story that illustrates the real value of discrimination. You may remember the devastating earthquake that struck the Indian state of Gujarat in January 2001. Thousands of people were killed, and many more were injured or lost their loved ones and homes as well as their hopes and dreams. Amma's ashram adopted and completely rebuilt three of the worst-hit villages. After the villages were reconstructed, Amma visited the area and met with the villagers there. One man told Amma that though he had lost his entire family and everything else in the earthquake, he was more determined than ever to become a successful businessman. Another man who had also been a merchant before the earthquake — and had met with a similar fate — told Amma that the disaster had revealed to him the fickle nature of worldly possessions and attachments, and his only remaining desire was to merge in God. Though both men had experienced the same fate, one man was still putting all his effort into achieving worldly happiness that could disappear at any moment. The other was able to use his discrimination to seek permanent peace and happiness.

The first chapter of the *Bhagavad Gita* is called *Arjuna Vishada Yoga*, or "The Yoga of Arjuna's Anguish." We may wonder how sorrow can become yoga (the process of uniting with God). If parents lose a child, they can take it in one of two ways. Either they can feel that they have lost everything and there is no point in going on any longer, or they can reflect on the truth of the changing nature of the world. They can ask themselves, "What is this? I thought my child would live long and bring me so much happiness. Now he is gone. What I thought was permanent has proven short-lived indeed. If I pin my hopes on such transient things, I am doomed to despair. Instead, let me depend on something permanent that will never betray me." By contemplating in this way, we can turn toward God. Thus, any sorrowful experience can become a means to bring us closer to God.

The Hindu scriptures tell us there are two paths open to each of us. One is called *preyo marga*, or the pursuit of material happiness, i.e. wealth, power, fame, etc. This path is a cycle that never ends; it will leave us perpetually bound in samsara (the cycle of birth and death). The second path is called *sreyo marga*, or the pursuit of ultimate happiness, i.e. knowing our own Divine Self. This path will lead us out of the cycle of birth and death and into eternal freedom.

This does not mean that in order to pursue ultimate happiness we should not have any material possessions, but we must be aware of the limitations of worldly objects. This awareness should impel us to aim for that which is limitless. That is only God, our own true nature.

To remind us that we neither bring anything into this world nor take anything with us when we leave, Amma often relates a story about the death of the Greek Emperor Alexander the Great.

As you all know, Alexander was a great warrior and ruler who had conquered nearly one third of the then-known world. He wanted to become the emperor of the entire world, but he fell sick with a terminal illness. A few days before his death, Alexander called his ministers and explained how he would like his body to be carried in the burial procession. He told them that he would like openings to be made on either side of his coffin, through which his hands should be kept hanging out, with the palms spread open. The ministers asked their lord why he wanted this to be done.

Alexander explained that, in this way, everyone would come to know that the "Great Alexander," who spent his whole life striving to possess and conquer the world, had left the world totally empty-handed. Therefore, they would understand how futile it is to spend one's life chasing after the world and its objects.

Discrimination means the capacity to distinguish between that which is permanent and that which is impermanent, to hold onto only the permanent, and to try to attain what is permanent. In the spiritual sense, only God, or the Atman, is permanent. Everything else is impermanent. The scriptures say that "The Atman was there in the past, it is here now, and it will be there in the future." That is why the Atman is called Truth. According to the Hindu scriptures, only that which exists—without growing, decaying, or changing at all—in the three periods of time (past, present, and future) can be called Truth. If anyone or anything in your life stands up to this test, that person or object can be called Truth. Otherwise, they are not the real Truth. When we practice *viveka* (discrimination), we will realize that nothing in the external world — whether object, person, or place — can pass this test. Then we will discover that many things we have been holding onto or trying to gain are not worth the trouble.

Amma wants us to understand the impermanence of the world and its objects. They are temporary and can never come with us after death.

So we can see that the power of discrimination is very important. We can use it to transform our weaknesses into a creative force, as well as to use our strengths in the most effective way. This will help us to become successful in all our life's endeavors, including our efforts to attain the ultimate success, Self-realization. ❖

CHAPTER 17

From Discrimination to Detachment

When we exercise our viveka in the right way, *vairagya* arises within us. Vairagya means detachment from all that is untrue, or impermanent. When we see that the people and objects in our life are not Truth, we will automatically become detached from them. This does not mean that we don't love them or care for them, but that we don't expect anything from them. In an ordinary relationship, the love we have for the other person is mostly dependent on what we get from them. If we don't get what we want from them, our love for that person diminishes. To quote Amma's example, we take good care of a cow as long as it continues to give us milk. When the cow stops giving milk, we will not hesitate to sell the cow, even to a butcher. This is the nature of ordinary, or worldly, love.

When detachment arises, the love we have for others is no longer dependent on what we get from them. We just love them for the sake of loving them. This detachment also applies to objects and possessions. If we have detachment, we will make the best use of the objects that are available to us. But if we lose something or if we cannot acquire it, this loss or lack will not disturb us at all.

There is a story that Aristotle once told his pupil Alexander the Great, "If you ever go to India, bring a yogi back to Greece with you." Many years later, when Alexander the Great was in the Himalayas, he came across a yogi seated on the ground. Remembering his teacher's request, Alexander approached the yogi and told him, "If you come with me, I will make you richer than a king. You will have your very own mansion and any number of servants to wait on your every desire."

Hearing Alexander's offer, the yogi politely declined, saying, "There is nothing in this world that I need or desire. If you want to help me, please just take two steps to the side so that I can enjoy the sun's rays." The yogi was utterly detached from the objects of the world. It did not matter to him whether he sat in a cave or a mansion. He was enjoying the bliss from within.

We may think that it is easy for a yogi living in the Himalayas to be detached, but for us, with all our responsibilities and possessions, it is impossible. But look at Amma. She has many more responsibilities than we have, and even though She attends to them with the utmost care and concern, She is perfectly detached. Someone once commented to Amma, "You have so many institutions and ashram centers. How does that make you feel?"

Amma replied, "Even though the peanut is inside the shell, it is not attached to the shell. Just like a snake molting its skin, Amma can discard all of this at any time. She is not attached to anything."

In life, we get some things and we lose some things. Nothing stays with us forever; objects and people will one day leave us, and if they do not, we will leave them — at least at the moment of death. If we are able to live life with detachment, our mind will be relatively calm, and our spiritual practices will not be disturbed by the difficulties and challenges of life. Only when we are attached to an object will it cause us misery. For example, suppose somebody vandalizes our neighbor's car. We might sympathize with them, but we will probably not get angry or upset. However, if the same thing were to happen to our car, we would be greatly disturbed. If we were very attached to the car, we might even get angry with God, asking how He could let this happen to us. The amount of suffering we experience when an object changes or is lost is directly proportional to our level of attachment to that object.

Once there was a miserly person. Even if he saw a penny lying in a sewage drain, he would pick it up. One day his neighbor phoned him at work to tell him that his house had been destroyed in a fire. Before telling him the news, the neighbor asked the miser to sit down, as he was sure that the miser would faint upon hearing of this loss. However, when the miser heard what the neighbor had to say, he started laughing. The neighbor was surprised and thought that the miser must have gone mad upon hearing this shocking news. He inquired to the miser, "Why are you laughing? Have you lost your mind?"

The miser replied, "No, I sold the house three days ago!"

The miser was able to laugh at the news because it was not his house anymore. If he had received the same news four days before, he would have reacted just as the neighbor expected him to. This is the freedom detachment gives us — we feel that the objects of the world, even those in our possession, do not belong to us. Therefore, we feel no attachment toward these objects (or people) and we are not troubled when they change or pass away.

Once there was a cowherd boy. Every day he would take the cows for grazing in the fields. After they were finished grazing, he would tie the cows to some trees or posts so they could get some rest. When the sun was low in the sky, he would untie the ropes, and the cows would start walking home. One day after the cows finished grazing, he brought them to the usual place where they rested, but he did not bother to tie them up; he knew they were creatures of habit and they would not go anywhere.

When he came back in the evening, he tried to get the cows to return home. But however much he tried, they would not move. Some had been lying down, and they all stood up, but they did not move. As the boy was a very intelligent cowherd, he understood what was happening. He went near some of the trees and pretended he was untying the ropes, even though on this day he had not tied them to the trees and thus did not have to untie any ropes. The cows did not know he hadn't tied them up. They were thinking, "Unless he unties our rope, how can we go anywhere?" After the boy pretended to untie the ropes, the cows started walking.

In the same way, our attachments are at the level of the mind. When I say that I am attached to my TV, it doesn't mean there is a rope connecting me to the TV. All our attachments — whether to our TV, house, car, relatives, or friends — are mental projections. Thus by making a strong mental resolve, we can overcome our attachments. Amma says, "Things are with you only for a short time. They belonged to someone else before you were here, and they will belong to someone else when you are gone. If your possessions were really yours, they would stay with you forever. In truth, nothing really belongs to you."

Knowing that one day everything will leave us, we should think that we are only a temporary custodian of all our possessions, appointed by God. Then, we will not be too much affected when an object or a person goes away from us. Since everything belongs to God, we will understand that He can take things or people away whenever he wants. The problem comes only when we think, "This is mine." This sense of possessiveness is one of the primary causes for our misery.

In reality, we are not attached to anything. The scriptures say, "Everything belongs to the Atman, but the Atman does not belong to anything or anyone — it is ever free, and you are that Atman." ❖

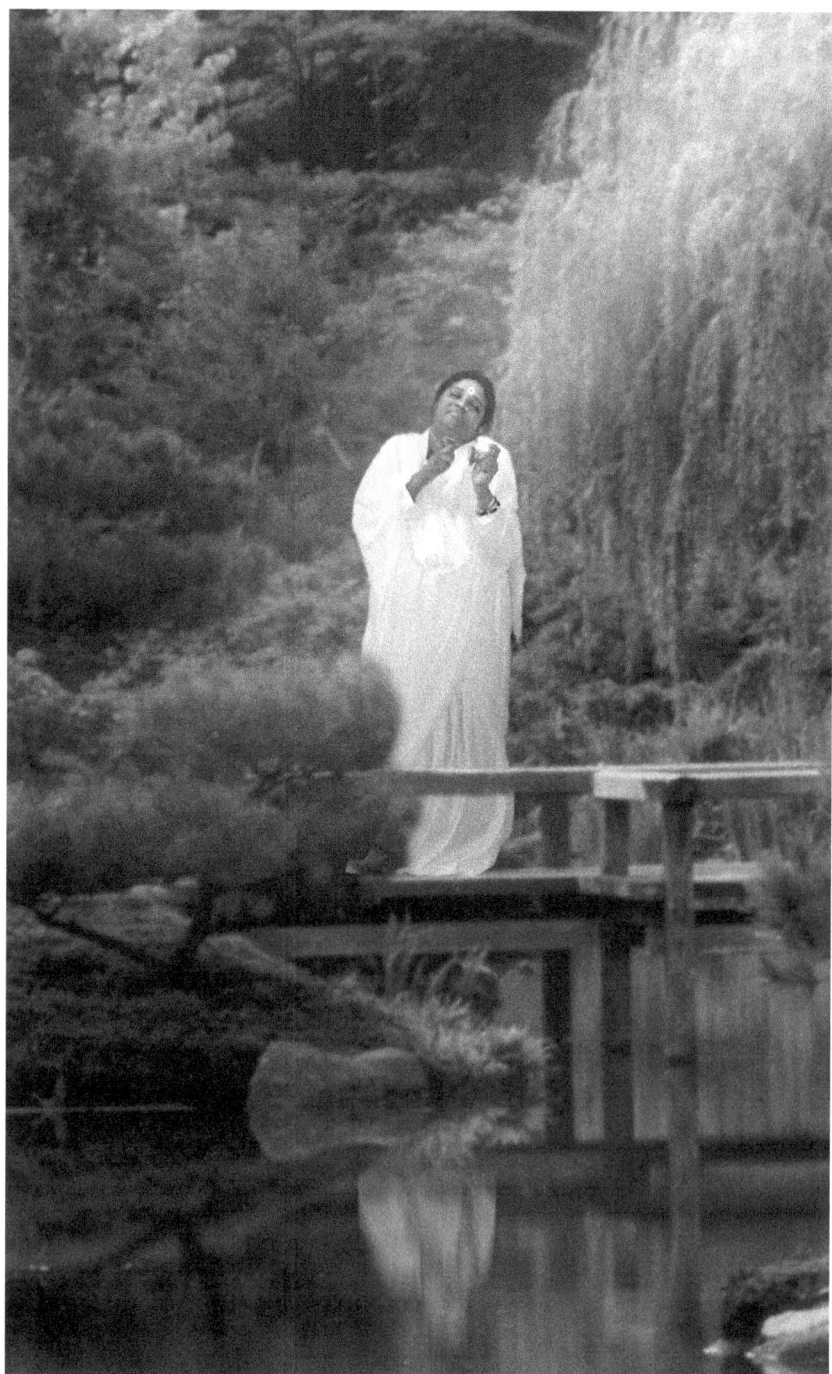

CHAPTER 18

Understanding the Nature of the World

If we want to save ourselves disappointment, we have to be prepared for all possible outcomes in any given situation. This is the logical approach to life. Amma gives us a very practical example. If we touch our finger to a flame, our finger burns. We don't get angry at the fire, nor do we hate it, but the next time we have to do something with fire, we prepare ourselves. We are careful not to touch the fire directly, as we don't want to burn our finger again. Because we changed the way we relate to it, the fire, which burned us once, can now be used to our benefit. Similarly, we all know the nature of the world. If things are not happening the way we want them to, we have to change the way we relate to the world.

Some people left the ashram a few years back, and we were all very upset. But Amma was not at all upset. She explained, "I don't expect anybody to stay with me until they die. Anybody can go at any time they want. I never expect anything. Even if all the swamis leave the ashram, I will continue to do what I have to do."

Amma is living in the same world in which we live, but the way we relate to the world is different from the way Amma relates to the world. If we want to be happy and peaceful, there is no other way except to change the way we are relating to the world.

A city was fraught with problems because of a burgeoning rat population. The citizens were outraged with the local government over their inability to control the problem. Yielding to the pressure of the voters, the mayor unveiled a new project called "Rat Eradication," but after a few months of concerted efforts, the mayor realized that it was not going to be an easy job. Frustrated by the lack of progress, the citizens resumed their protests. Hoping to lower their expectations, the mayor renamed the project, "Rat Control." Soon he discovered that it was as impossible to control the rats as it was to eradicate them. The people again took to the streets, and the desperate mayor announced his new plan. He called it, "Co-existing with Rats."

Similarly, it is not possible to eliminate all the problems in the world and in our life. We may be able to control problems to a certain extent; whatever we cannot control, we have to learn to accept.

A man who had been having many problems went to a Vedic astrologer to ask about his future. The astrologer told him, "Oh, you're going through a very bad period. You have been under the influence of Rahu for 15 years, and you have three more years to go. It will continue to be very difficult for you."

"What happens after that?"

The astrologer gave him a sympathetic look. "After that you'll be under the influence of Jupiter for 12 years. For most people that would have been an improvement. But yours is a special case. Jupiter is poorly placed in your chart; it will also create problems for you."

"And after Jupiter?"

"After Jupiter, you'll be in Saturn for 19 years. This will give you even more problems than the previous years."

The man said, "What about after that? Will my problems finally be over?"

The astrologer said, "After that, your problems will be no problem for you, as you will have gotten used to all sorts of problems."

Amma says that in times of crisis and frustration, we should try to count our blessings rather than our problems. There are always many things for which we can be thankful to God. Amma says that we are so focused on complaining about the things we do not have that we lose sight of the good things we already have.

When we go to sleep at night, what is the guarantee that we will wake up in the morning? We don't even know what is going to happen the next moment. Human life is so fragile. Anything can happen at any time. In Gujarat in 2001, everything was calm just a few minutes before the devastating earthquake; five minutes later many homes, hopes, and lives were destroyed. Our life is like that; it is so fragile. If a particular nerve twists, I won't be able to lift my arm. It is a matter of a second.

What can we do in such a world? We should try to be happy with what we have. Of course, there is nothing wrong in trying to get more. There is no guarantee that we will get it, but if we do, let us be thankful to God. Even for waking up in the morning, we should give thanks to God. Every day, every moment of our life is a blessing from God.

I remember a story. One day all the insects went before God to air their grievances about life on earth. The mosquitoes explained to God, "Lord, you have given us the proboscis to sting and suck blood from human beings, you have created human beings with flesh and plenty of blood, and you have given us a tiny body and wings so that we can fly away when there is danger. You have been so merciful and kind to us. But there is one problem: Why did you create our enemy, the wind? Whenever we are about to enjoy our hearty meal, the wind blows, and we have to fly away for dear life. So why can you not remove the wind from the earth?"

The Lord said, "My children, you are all dear to me. I cannot decide the case without the presence of the accused. Bring the wind here, and I will decide." But the mosquito knew that if the wind came, the mosquito would have to leave. Instead of going and inviting the wind, the mosquito turned to some of her friends.

The mosquito said to the other bugs, "Dear brothers and sisters, you are all happy. You drink human beings' blood to your heart's content. But our case is really pitiable. The moment the wind approaches us, we have to flee. Do you have any suggestion or tips for us?"

One of the bugs replied, "You think that we have it so good. Listen to our situation. We are bed bugs. We have no wings to fly like you. We want to approach the Lord to give us wings to fly. Or we are going to ask the Lord to create humans without eyes because even if we hide in a corner of the bed, humans somehow find us and crush us or kill us with bug spray."

The biting fly chimed in, "Our sufferings are indescribable. We sit on a human being to drink the blood, and he gives us a hard slap. We are finished; our life is gone. Somehow, we often manage to escape. Then we have to starve for many days. Though we are fond of blood, we cannot get a single drop. We want to pray to God to create human beings without hands."

The Lord heard their complaints very patiently but kept quiet. What could He say? Even God cannot decide such cases; He simply has to keep quiet because He knows the nature of creation. Can you imagine the condition of human beings if the desires of all the mosquitoes, bugs, and flies were fulfilled?

Amma says not all difficulties can be removed. Willingly or unwillingly, we have come to this world. The best we can do is to try to understand the nature of the world. This understanding, coupled with our faith in God or in a Satguru like Amma, will give us the strength to face our problems with a positive outlook.

Problems exist for us mainly because of our mind. It is said that the mind alone is the cause of liberation and bondage; the mind alone is the cause of sorrow and happiness.

Most types of information are not essential to our existence. Just because you have not studied calculus, you are not going to be unhappy. Similarly, if you want to study botany, you can study it; if you don't want to study botany, it is not going to have a negative effect on your life. There are many unhappy botanists and mathematicians. But everyone has to study spiritual principles in order to lead a happy and peaceful life. For this reason, spiritual study was an important aspect of education in the ancient Indian tradition. These days the scriptures are considered out of date. We think we don't need to know anything about spirituality to succeed in life. In fact, we need spiritual understanding today more than ever — our moral and ethical values have fallen dramatically as a direct result of its absence. This lack of values is creating problems both for society and the individual that were unthinkable until the recent past. Without understanding the spiritual principles, we will always be miserable and depressed, and there will be no harmony in society.

Having a firm grasp on the essential principles of spirituality gives us strength, not physical strength but emotional strength. We may be physically very strong, even Herculean, but when it comes to facing problems in life, our physical strength will not be very helpful. In most times of crisis, nothing is going to help us except our own emotional strength, which arises from a true understanding of the nature of the world.

Amma says, "If we feed our body with junk food, we will have a sick body. Similarly, if we feed our mind with negative thoughts, we will have a sick mind. Just as our body needs good food every day, our mind needs positive spiritual thoughts to be strong and healthy."

This is not to say that knowledge about spirituality is enough by itself. Many of us already have a great deal of spiritual information, but as long as it remains as mere information, it will not really benefit us. Only when we put our knowledge into practice does it really benefit us.

If we eat but the food is not digested, how are we going to get nourishment? It is not the food we eat, but the food that is digested that gives us strength. Similarly, we may read many spiritual books and listen to many satsangs (spiritual discourses), but if we are not able to put those teachings into practice, we will not get the benefit.

That is why Amma always gives importance to spiritual practices and to the assimilation of spiritual principles into our daily life. If we approach life in the right way, the difficult situations we face can help us to strengthen our mind. Our mind is like a muscle — it expands or contracts depending on how much or how little we exercise it.

The scriptures say, "*Panditaha na anusochanthi.*" This means, "Wise persons do not grieve." The scriptures are telling us that the solution for grief is wisdom. Wisdom is *jnana*, or the knowledge that "I am not the body, the mind, the intellect, or the ego. I am one with the Supreme Consciousness." Only people who are established in this wisdom can avoid sorrow.

The greater the depth of our assimilation and understanding of the Truth, the fewer grievances we will have. When we realize our oneness with the Divine Consciousness, all our grievances will disappear — even if we have problems, it will not be a problem for us.

Unlike our happiness, the happiness of a Self-realized person is not dependent on any condition. Amma does not depend on anything in this world for Her happiness, contentment, or peace of mind — it is unconditional. Our situation is different, isn't it? Our peace of mind is dependent on so many things from the world. If certain conditions are met, we will be happy. If they are not met, we will be unhappy. We think that only if we get a good job, or only if we have a good family, or only if we get married, will we feel truly happy. Of course, these are all important for us, but there is no guarantee that such things will always make us happy.

Amma says that many people feel that unless they are married, they will never feel complete, but later they say, "Now that I am married, I'm finished." If we analyze it closely, we will see that this approach to life — pinning our hopes on any external goal, object, or person — is never going to make us truly happy and content.

Only the science of spirituality will help us in this regard. A spiritually educated person has an armor of knowledge that will prevent him or her from being affected negatively by the ups and downs of life. If life can be compared to a battlefield, then spiritual knowledge is the armor that will prevent us from getting hurt. Various weapons may still strike us, but they will not penetrate our armor. We will be unaffected by the assaults.

Similarly, even for a Satguru, there will be problems in life. They may have even more problems than you or I. For us it may be more than enough just to take care of one small family. Consider Amma's case. She has to take care of thousands, even millions of families. Many devotees want Amma to find a spouse for their child, or they want Amma to settle a family dispute, or a problem between the husband and wife. Many times, Amma takes steps to see that the devotees' desires are fulfilled, even without their verbally asking Her for anything.

When my younger sister attained the proper age, Amma found a boy for her, and Amma performed the marriage. One day Amma called me in Australia where I was conducting programs and said, "Amma has arranged your sister's marriage; it is going to take place at the ashram on such and such a date." I was not at all worried about my family members. I had not given any thought to the matter of my sister finding a husband. Amma took care of that. This is just an example; in a similar manner She is taking care of thousands of families all over the world.

Thus, we can see that a Satguru has many more responsibilities than we do, yet is never overwhelmed or stressed in any way. This is because the Satguru has the proper understanding about life. Only this spiritual wisdom gives us a permanent solution to our problems—that is, the determination to solve any problem that can be solved and the strength to accept with equanimity any problem that cannot be solved. It is up to us whether we want to study mathematics, botany, or almost any other subject, but if we want to be truly happy, we have no choice but to gain spiritual wisdom.

The scriptures say:

kasya sukham na karōthi viragaḥ

Which person who is detached will not be happy?

If we analyze our life carefully, we will find that many of the objects we have spent so much time pursuing have given us more unhappiness than happiness. Even to gain any happiness at all from the world, we have to put in so much effort.

Suppose we want to buy an expensive sports car. We think we will be really happy once it is ours. First, we have to work hard to earn the money, and once the car is purchased, we have to work hard to maintain it. After some time, it starts to break down, and eventually, the repair costs will be greater than the original cost of the car. Even before that happens, it may be destroyed in an accident. When we think about how much happiness and satisfaction we received from owning the car, versus how much trouble it gave us, we may wonder if it was really worth the effort. Yet even if we realize that such pursuits involve more trouble and less happiness, we still chase after worldly objects. This is because of our inability to overcome our attraction for them. Even before our car is towed away, we will be thinking about the new model we are going to acquire.

To expect to receive permanent happiness from impermanent things is quite illogical. Amma says, "Trying to gain permanent happiness from the world is like trying to roll up the sky and tuck it in your armpit — it will never happen. Unless we turn inward, we can never get permanent or eternal happiness."

We may feel that we will be happy after we have fulfilled certain desires. We may think we have only 10 desires, and once we have fulfilled them we will be happy and content. However, if we ever manage to fulfill all 10, we will be surprised to discover that the list of 10 has grown to 15. Then we are sure that if we fulfill just those 15 desires, we will finally be at peace. And if we are somehow able to fulfill all 15, we will find that the list has grown to 20. Trying to fulfill all these desires takes time; finally we grow old and eventually die in the process. The promise of worldly happiness is like trying to reach the foot of a rainbow. No matter how far we travel, we find it is always still further away.

Why is it that all human beings instinctively seek joy? This innate urge arises because human beings have come from the Supreme Being who is of the nature of infinite bliss. This experience is embedded in the human consciousness, though we are not consciously aware of it, and hence we all deeply desire to experience it again. Thus, the yearning for joy is inherent in every human being, and consciously or unconsciously, humanity strives toward this end alone. Just as water always flows down toward the sea and a bird will always try to escape its cage, it is the nature of all things to struggle to return to their natural state. The purpose of the scriptures and of the Satguru's life is to show human beings the path to return to their natural state, which is infinite and eternal joy.

However, we are all looking for permanent happiness in the wrong place. We feel it is easier to search in the world outside because our mind is extroverted to begin with. The outside objects provide only a reflection of true happiness, but we take the reflection to be the real thing. We think that it is bright outside and dark within, but Amma knows it is the other way around. She is slowly guiding us to turn our vision within to find real success.

Only if we see the inherent defects in the dream of worldly happiness will we be able to withdraw ourselves. However, our awareness level is so low that even if we are informed about the defects, we do not always turn away from the object. For example, in every advertisement about cigarettes they are required to say that smoking is injurious to health. The information used to be in very small print, but nowadays, if you see a bulk package of cigarettes in the West, it will say SMOKING KILLS in big block letters across one side of the package. Still, many people buy cigarettes with this packaging. There is a joke about a chain smoker. He told his friend that there was an attractive new advertisement for his preferred brand of cigarette that was running in the daily newspaper, but the whole effect was ruined by the statutory warning saying that smoking is injurious to health. "Finally," the smoker told his friend, "I got so fed up because of this that I just gave it up."

The friend was surprised. "You gave up smoking?"

"No," said the chain smoker. "I gave up reading the newspaper."

Even if the defect is clearly mentioned, we are unable to withdraw from the object. What can be said, then, about the defects of worldly happiness, which does not carry a warning label?

I am not trying to paint a pessimistic picture of life. The view of the scriptures, the view of spirituality, is neither pessimistic nor optimistic — it is realistic. Once we have truly understood the nature of the world, it will be easy for us to cultivate detachment. In this way even if we are immersed in worldly responsibilities and relationships, we will not be buffeted by the vicissitudes and hardships of life. We will know that the real source of happiness lies not outside but within us, and we will seek refuge in That alone.

Once there was a kingdom with a very unusual system of government. Whoever wanted to become the king was accepted under one condition. After five years, he would be exiled to a deserted island inhabited only by poisonous snakes and wild animals, where he would be sure to die. Many were attracted by the five years of life in the lap of luxury, and there was a long waiting list to become the king. However, immediately after being crowned, each new king was seen to be more depressed and morose than the one before. Knowing that their days as a king were numbered, and that beyond that only suffering and death awaited them, none of the kings could enjoy even a single hour of their five years as lord of the land. The citizens of the country were even considering revising their system of government when they realized the latest king was different. He was always smiling and laughing, giving gifts, pardoning criminals, and hosting great celebrations. Even as the years passed and the end of the king's reign approached, his enthusiasm and good cheer never faded. Finally, the day came when it was time to give up the throne and go alone to the deserted island. The palace guards stormed the king's chambers expecting a fight, as was usually necessary on the day the king was sent into exile. But this king was already standing by the door, and he was still all smiles as he walked out of the city and onto the boat that would take him to the deserted island.

As the king was boarding the boat, one of the palace guards asked him, "Knowing your fate, why were you always smiling? How can you be so happy even now?"

"The very first day I became the king," he confided, "I sent ships of men to clear the island of all the dangerous animals and unpleasant vegetation. When that was finished, I sent more men to build a palace with beautiful gardens that makes the palace I am leaving seem like a dungeon. I am always smiling because I know that even though I am being sent away from here, a much better life awaits me."

Just like the king in the story, we should not waste our energy brooding over the fact that we are here only for a short time.

Instead, we should put our efforts toward attaining that which is permanent — the state of God-realization, or realizing our True Self. ❖

CHAPTER 19

Integrated Growth Is Real Growth

When we say growth, we are usually referring to the growth of the body. All living beings begin their life in a small form, and over time, grow bigger and stronger. Other than humans, the growth of all living beings is limited to growth on the physical level. Unless they are trained by human beings to perform a simple, specific function, animals cannot do anything different from their ancestors. Today, the cat cries "meow" just as its ancestors did thousands of years ago. Donkeys also bray exactly as their ancestors used to. A donkey cannot sing like a human being, though a human being may bray like a donkey. Human beings have evolved. In the beginning, we were gesturing, then grunting and making primitive sounds, and then communicating in a basic language. Afterwards, we started writing, singing, and even emailing.

The history of human evolution is the story of our growth on four different levels — physical, mental, intellectual and spiritual. There was a time when muscle power was considered superior to all other qualities of human beings. With the technological revolution and the development of education and civilization, intelligence is valued most in today's world.

Now, people use their intellect, rather than brute force, to try to get ahead in the world. Is that a sign of real growth? Unless we grow on all four planes simultaneously and systematically, we cannot claim we are really evolving.

Amma often says, "Our body is growing in all directions, but our mind is not." This is because everybody grows physically just by getting enough food and sleep — it doesn't require any additional effort on our part. Neither is it possible to improve on the involuntary processes of the body, as they are not conscious processes. It is not possible for us to become better at using our liver, hone our blood-circulatory skills, or improve our motor-neuron functions. We can only indirectly improve these functions by maintaining our health. But when awareness is involved in a function, we can improve on it.

For example, if we make a conscious effort, it is possible for us to be more patient, more discriminative, and more compassionate. This shows that if we want to grow mentally, intellectually, or spiritually, awareness is the key factor. Although physical growth has its limits, potential for growth at the other three levels is unlimited. Of course, while the infinite potential of the Self is present in all of us, the degree to which this potential is manifested will vary. For example, both a 100-watt bulb and a 10-watt bulb are illuminated by the power of electricity. Because of the condition of the instrument, the 100-watt bulb will shine much brighter than the 10-watt bulb.

Growth on these levels is not a natural process. Conscious, persistent self-effort is essential. For example, we can say that butter is present in milk in a latent form. However, only if we churn the milk for the required length of time can we get butter. Similarly, if we continuously put forth effort, there is no limit to how much we can love others or how compassionate we can become. We can cultivate all-encompassing love and compassion thereby embracing all of creation. Amma is a living example of how much our heart can expand. This is called mental growth.

Remember, according to Vedanta, the mind is the seat of the emotions and the intellect is the decision-making faculty. So when we talk about mental growth, it includes developing emotional maturity as well as cultivating positive qualities like unconditional love, compassion, kindness, patience, etc. All virtues are an indication of a growing, healthy mind.

There is room for enormous growth at the intellectual level as well. We can go on studying about the universe from subatomic particles to the ever-expanding galaxies. The fields of study available for humans are so numerous that the average person cannot even name them all. In the field of physics alone, the available knowledge is so vast that it is no longer possible for a single student to learn everything there is to know about physics in his or her lifetime — he or she has to specialize in one small area of knowledge. Thus, our capacity for intellectual growth is virtually infinite — it is limited only by our life span.

However, the actual yardstick of our intellectual growth is the development of our power of discrimination. When we go to college, our intellect develops significantly, but whether or not we decide to use that development in a righteous way depends on how much discrimination we have acquired along with it. The knowledge of how to split an atom can either be used to generate vast amounts of electricity or to make warheads that can reduce the whole earth to ashes. If we have developed the power of discrimination, we will not use our intellectual capacities to create more suffering but to reduce it. By finding ways to benefit those around us and society as a whole, we reduce the suffering of others. By using our discrimination to differentiate between the permanent and the impermanent, we reduce the suffering in our own life.

The fourth level of growth is spiritual growth. If positive qualities denote mental growth and the power of discrimination determines intellectual growth, the criterion for spiritual growth is the expansion of the sense of "I." At present, most of us are conditioned to think of ourselves as a physical body with mental and intellectual faculties. Our broadest definition of self includes our family, profession and country. We should recognize the limitations of our present conditioning and try to gradually expand the boundaries until we can embrace all of creation as our True Self. In fact, our real nature is Brahman, which is infinite, omniscient, omnipotent, and all-pervading. As such, there is no limit to how much we can grow spiritually. When we realize the nature of our True Self, we realize that we are, indeed, infinite.

A Satguru is one who has attained this goal and can help others to attain it. Of course, all of us have the potential to reach the same state as Amma because essentially we are all one and the same Consciousness. That is why Amma addresses all Her children as "*Omkara divya porule*," meaning, "the essence of Om." The Satguru starts working on us at the mental and intellectual levels and slowly leads us to our eternal home of everlasting bliss. At the mental level, he or she helps us to overcome our negativities and to develop virtuous qualities. At the intellectual level, the Satguru makes us understand what is eternal and what is ephemeral as well as how to discriminate between the two. At the spiritual level, the limitless love and compassion of the Satguru dissolves our ego and makes us realize our oneness with the Satguru and with all of creation.

The Guru's job is primarily to help us grow mentally and spiritually. There are many examples of wealthy people who were focused on accumulating more wealth for themselves and their family members until they met Amma. After meeting Amma, they have given up many of the comforts they were used to. They now lead lives in a spirit of renunciation while donating their time and resources to helping those in need. This is an example of mental growth. There are also examples of people who used to have a fiery temper and would get very upset over small things. After meeting Amma, the same people are calm and composed even under difficult circumstances.

There was a doctor who used to come to the ashram and administer medical treatment free of charge. However, he had a very short temper, and he would often scold the patients ferociously. The ashram residents would complain to Amma that he was so cruel that they were afraid to go to him even if they were sick. Amma told the doctor about the complaints.

He admitted that he had a bad temper. He explained that he had struggled to overcome it, but that all his efforts had been in vain. Amma told the doctor, "My son, Amma can help you overcome your anger, but you have to promise Her one thing." The doctor looked hesitant. Amma told him not to worry, that what She was going to ask him to do was definitely within his power. Hearing Amma's reassuring words, the doctor agreed to do whatever Amma asked. Giving him a framed picture of Her, protected by a glass pane, Amma said, "My son, whenever you feel angry with someone, Amma wants you to hit this picture as hard as you can." The doctor was shocked by Amma's instructions, but since he had made the promise to Amma, he resolved to do his best.

The next day, the doctor found himself getting angry with the patients as usual. Each time he lost his temper, he waited for the patient to leave and then he very gently hit Amma's picture. After a few days, Amma asked him how he was doing managing his anger. He told Her that there had been some improvement, but he was still losing his temper. Amma asked him if he was hitting Her picture as hard as he could. The doctor admitted he was only gently hitting the picture, as he could not bring himself to really pound on a picture of Amma. Amma reminded him he had made a promise and told him again that next time he got angry, he must hit the picture as hard as he could.

The doctor returned to the clinic resolved to be careful not to get angry. He reminded himself that if he got angry he would have to hit Amma's photo very hard, which he could not imagine doing. By force of habit, the next day he badly scolded a patient for not following his instructions. After the patient left, he went over to Amma's picture hanging on the wall. Bracing himself, he hit Amma's picture very hard, breaking the glass over the photo. Immediately, realizing what he had done, he was devastated. He felt so remorseful that he could not even eat for three days.

After that, a great change came over the doctor. His patients even began praising his remarkable degree of kindness and patience. A few months later, Amma released him from his promise with a warning that he should always be careful about his temper. It might seem as though She took an extreme measure in this case, but Amma knew it was the only way to help the doctor overcome his bad temper. Thus, Amma helped him to grow mentally.

Spiritual growth means imbibing spiritual principles such as detachment, selflessness, and surrender. Amma embodies all these qualities perfectly. We can cultivate these qualities by observing Amma, and trying to follow Her example and Her instructions.

Many years back, the authorities at a temple in one of the villages near the ashram asked me to come and hold a program there. As usual, I asked Amma's permission before giving them an answer. Amma agreed for me to go, and we scheduled the satsang to take place the following week.

The day of the scheduled satsang, I arrived at the temple at 4:30 in the afternoon. No one was there. I wasn't worried because the program was not scheduled to begin until 5:00 p.m. I waited patiently. However, by 5:00, no one had yet arrived to attend the satsang. I decided to wait for some more time before beginning. 5:15, 5:30, and 5:45 came and went, and still no one had come.

By 6:00, two people, who appeared to have come solely for the purpose of worshipping at the temple, saw me seated there and sat down to hear what I had to say. When they sat down, I began chanting the opening prayers. Usually the prayers take just a minute or two, but hoping more people would arrive to hear the satsang, I added verse after verse, in between secretly peeking out to see if more people had come. In this way, I extended the opening prayers to 10 minutes.

Finally, I saw a group of people approaching, and I concluded the prayers. After I began speaking, however, I saw that these people, too, had not really come to hear me speak. They stood in the hall for a few minutes, and then they went inside the temple to pray. I had prepared a long speech, but under the circumstances, I spoke only for a few minutes. Then I closed my eyes and started singing bhajans. I kept singing with my eyes closed until I heard the temple priests preparing to begin the *arati* (worship performed by waving burning camphor before the image of the deity). By this time there were about 20 people in the hall — whether they had come for the program or just for the temple arati, I didn't know. After the temple arati was complete, I sang Amma's arati and then returned to the ashram.

Very upset with the way the program had gone, I went to Amma with a long face. I knew that Amma had known, of course, how many people would attend the program. I told Her that under those circumstances She should not have given permission for me to go. She responded, "Amma told you to give satsang, not to count the number of people who attended. Even though people did not come to the temple for the program, it was being broadcast on the temple loudspeakers. You don't know how many people were listening inside their houses. Many of them were waiting to hear the satsang. You should have started the program at the scheduled time and given the full satsang."

Amma went on to say, "If Amma tells you to do something, you should learn to do it without worrying about the result." When Amma told me that, I realized my mistake. Whenever the Satguru tells us to do something, there is definitely a purpose behind it, even if it is not clear to us at the time.

Many years later, during one of my visits to Colombia, I was scheduled to conduct a Devi Puja in Bogota. Around noon I went to the hall to help set up for the program. Even though I was not scheduled to begin until 6:00 p.m., people started assembling from 2:00 onward. The setup was complete by 3:00, and I returned to the house where I was staying. On my way out, I saw that there was already quite a large crowd in the hall. I assumed there was another function going on that afternoon. When I returned to the hall just before 6:00 p.m., I was very surprised to see a long line of people outside. My first thought was that there was some problem inside the hall and everyone had been asked to wait outside. But when I entered the hall, I saw that it was completely full. The people were standing outside because there was no more room inside. I thought there must have been some mistake in the advertisement for the program and that everyone expected that Amma Herself was going to be there.

I immediately spoke to one of the program's organizers and asked him whether there had been any mistake in the advertisement. He said, "No," and admitted he was also very surprised at the turnout. I was starting to get nervous — if all these people were expecting to see Amma, how could I possibly satisfy them? I could only give a talk, sing some bhajans, and conduct the puja. I felt totally helpless. I began praying, "Amma, how am I going to make these people happy? By my own power, I cannot do it. Only through Your grace will these people feel satisfied with this program."

Praying thus, I began the program as planned. I gave a talk, sang some bhajans and conducted the puja. However, I did not feel I was doing it — I felt as though through me, someone else was conducting the program. Though it felt like five minutes to me, the program took three hours. During that time, not one person left the hall. At the end of the program, I was surrounded. People rushed forward to touch me or touch their jewelry to me, saying they wanted to absorb some of the spiritual energy that was radiating from me. I was very surprised at their behavior. How could they get such a feeling from me? Then I realized it was purely Amma's grace.

When I told Amma about this incident, She said, "If you make yourself hollow, Amma can enter into you totally. Because you felt so helpless, you were able to surrender completely to Amma. That allowed Amma's energy to flow through you." Thus, if we are able to perform all our actions with the right spiritual understanding, we can become a perfect instrument to receive divine grace.

When I compare the program in Bogota with the program I conducted in the village near the ashram, I can see that Amma has helped me over the years to cultivate a better understanding of spiritual principles.

If we do not have intellectual maturity, we may not know the right action to perform. If we don't have mental maturity, we may not be able to find it within ourselves to perform the right action. And it is spiritual maturity that helps us to perform that action without being attached to the result. Thus, spiritual maturity is the foundation of all other aspects of growth. Even if we have intellectual and mental maturity, if we are attached to the results of our actions, we can get frustrated or depressed and lose our enthusiasm to serve the world and to persist in our spiritual practices. That is why integrated growth is so important.

Instead of simply growing physically, we should try to grow mentally, intellectually and spiritually as well. Only then will we be able to fulfill the purpose of this human birth. ❖

CHAPTER 20

Why Venus Is Hotter Than Mercury: The Importance of Receptivity

Our aim in coming to Amma should not be simply to fulfill our worldly desires — that would be like going to the king who is ready to give us his entire kingdom and asking for a carrot. Amma is ready to lead us to the ultimate goal of life, and we should not settle for anything less. However, in order to receive what Amma is offering us, we need to become receptive.

Amma is constantly guiding us and giving us what we need, but we don't get the full benefit of what She is giving due to our lack of receptivity. Mere physical closeness to the Guru is not enough; it is our receptivity that is most important.

In the solar system, Mercury is the closest planet to the sun, so logically it should also be the hottest. Actually, Venus is the hottest. Why is this so? It is because there is something special about the atmosphere surrounding Venus that makes it absorb more heat from the sun. In the same way, it is not just proximity to the Guru that counts but also the receptivity of the disciple.

If we lack the proper receptivity, we will not hear the Guru's words as they are expressed. They will always be colored and twisted by our own views and tendencies. Each person will interpret the Guru's words in his or her own way.

For example, when Amma gives darshan, She whispers different things in each person's ear—either in the native language of that person or in Her own native tongue of Malayalam. For example, She might say, "Mon kutta," meaning, "Darling son," or, "Mutte, mutte, mutte," meaning, "My precious child, my precious child."

But regardless of the language Amma is speaking, if there are 10 people, they will hear 10 different things. One person came to me and said he heard Amma whispering, "Tomorrow, tomorrow, tomorrow," in his ear. This was because he was hoping that he would be successful in his job interview the next day. Another woman was feeling guilty about her bad habits, so when Amma said, "My daughter, daughter, daughter," she said that she had heard "Naughty, naughty, naughty." Another man had purchased a bunch of bananas to offer to Amma, but he had forgotten them in his room. When he went for darshan, Amma said into his ear, "Ponnu mone, ponnu mone," meaning, "My beloved son," but somehow he heard it as, "Banana, banana, banana." Because of the preoccupations in each of these people's minds, they were not able to hear what Amma was trying to tell them.

Once, a 92-year-old man went to the doctor to get a physical examination. A few days later, the doctor saw the old man walking down the street with a beautiful young woman hanging onto his arm. The doctor was shocked and commented to the man, "Wow! You're really doing great, aren't you?"

The old man replied, "Just doing what you said, doctor: 'Get a hot mama and be cheerful.' Isn't that right?"

The doctor said, "No, that's not what I said! I said, 'You've got a heart murmur, so be careful.'"

Like this, the true meaning of the Master's words is often obscured by our own preferences, fears, and desires.

If this is our situation, then the Master cannot really help us. In order to benefit from the Master's words, we have to become as open and receptive as possible to what is really being said — as open and receptive as an innocent child.

There is a story about four friends. Three of the four friends would always side against the fourth in various arguments. One day during the course of a conversation, the fourth friend brought up a very valid point. As usual, the first three friends disdainfully disputed his idea. The fourth friend became so frustrated and sad that he started praying aloud to God, "Oh Lord, please show my friends a sign to prove that I am right." Immediately dark clouds began to gather overhead in what had been a crystal clear sky. The fourth friend pointed to the sky and said, "See, God has sent a sign that I am right!" The three friends scoffed at his claim, saying it was purely coincidental. The fourth friend became even more frustrated and pleaded to God to send an even stronger sign to convince his friends. Immediately the air was filled with thunder, and lightning flashed across the darkening sky. The fourth friend happily exclaimed, "Now there can be no doubt. God is on my side!"

The three friends were still unimpressed. "Oh, that's nothing. Where dark clouds gather, thunder and lightning are common," they shrugged.

The fourth friend desperately cried out to God, "Oh Lord, please give them an indisputable sign that you are with me!"

In response, a deep voice boomed out from above, "Lo, you must listen to your friend. His point is correct."

Upon hearing the voice of God, the three friends said, "So, God is on your side. But it's still three against two."

This story shows that some people will cling to their own ideas no matter how ridiculous or impractical; they are not at all open or receptive. Even if Amma Herself gives advice to such people, they will go their own way. This is why Amma says that it is easy to wake someone who is asleep, but it is very difficult to wake someone who is pretending to be asleep. Let us try not to be like the three friends in the story. We should always try to be open and receptive to what Amma is trying to teach us. If we think that we know everything, we will not be able to learn anything. ❖

CHAPTER 21

How to Develop True Devotion

Developing and increasing devotion to God, to our Guru, or to our spiritual goal is very important for our spiritual progress. Devotion to the Guru and devotion to God are one and the same. A Satguru is one with God. Even though he or she has a human form, the Satguru does not have the feeling of individuality or "I am so and so, and I have done such and such." The universal power of God works through the Satguru. So whatever comes from the Satguru is coming from God. Whenever Amma or any Mahatma says, "me," or "I," — for example, when Lord Krishna says in the *Bhagavad Gita*, "I am the basis of everything" — they are not referring to their body or to their particular form but to the Supreme Consciousness in which they are established.

Amma says that when we are developing devotion, we should be sure that it is *tattva bhakti*, or devotion based on right understanding and knowledge. Otherwise, our devotion will not be steady. We will have a strong feeling of devotion when things are going well in our life, but when something bad happens to us, our devotion will decline. When we have devotion based on knowledge, we will pray to God because we love God and we want to realize the Truth. We will not see God as an agent to fulfill our desires.

Tattva bhakti means knowing that whatever happens to us, whether good or bad, it is a result of our own past actions in this or previous lifetimes. It means understanding that if bad things happen to us, it is not out of God's lack of compassion, and if good things happen to us, that does not mean that God favors us. It's not like that. Everything that is happening is according to a person's own prarabdha. In this process, God is only a witness. Amma says, "Don't identify your devotion with the experiences that are happening to you. All your experiences are created by your own past actions. God has nothing to do with this. He has laid down a set of cosmic laws. If you follow those laws, you will have good experiences, and if you transgress those laws, you will have correspondingly bad experiences. Of course, there are some difficulties that can be removed by praying sincerely. However, other experiences cannot be avoided. In that case, we should pray for the strength to face these difficulties with equanimity of mind."

This does not mean we can blame everything on our prarabdha. Suppose I go and beat someone up. When the police come and take me to jail, I cannot blame my prarabdha. I know very well I should not beat someone up and that if I do, I will be punished. Having then beaten someone up, how can I blame my prarabdha when I go to jail? That is not prarabdha; it is the immediate result of an action I performed.

Our prarabdha is responsible for what happens in spite of our effort. If we climb a tree and then jump down onto the ground, we know it is very likely we will break our leg. If we then jump, and we do break our leg, we cannot say it was our prarabdha to break our leg. If we don't break our leg, however, then we can say that is a result of our good prarabdha. In other words, there are some general rules to life on earth. If the general rule does not apply to us in a certain situation, we can think that this is because of our good prarabdha. But we cannot put the blame on prarabdha for everything. If in spite of our sincere study and hard work, we still score poorly on an exam, then we can say it is our prarabdha. If we fail to study, we cannot blame prarabdha for our poor results.

I remember there was a devotee who was with Amma for many years. Amma gave him many wonderful experiences. Despite those memorable experiences, he was not able to develop steadfast devotion to Amma, and finally he stopped coming to see Her. We can learn a great deal from his story.

When Amma began manifesting *Krishna Bhava*, some people recognized Amma's divinity immediately. Others were very skeptical. They questioned how Lord Krishna could manifest in a human body.

One among the skeptics was not an atheist. He was actually a devotee of Lord Krishna. Whenever there was an auspicious occasion such as a birthday or a wedding, people would invite this devotee to their home to read aloud from the *Srimad Bhagavatam*, a sacred text that describes the divine play of Lord Krishna.

His friends, who had already seen Amma during Krishna Bhava, told him to go and see Amma as he was a devotee of Lord Krishna. He refused to go. He was not at all ready to believe that Lord Krishna would manifest in the body of this young woman.

His friends kept insisting that he meet Amma. Finally, he agreed, but he said he wanted proof that Amma was manifesting Lord Krishna before he would believe it.

One Krishna Bhava day, Amma was giving darshan to Her devotees at the ashram. Suddenly, She came out of the temple and started walking without telling anybody where She was going. The devotees were very surprised at Her sudden departure. Many people simply followed Her. Amma kept on walking and walking; She was walking so fast that everyone had to run to keep pace with Her.

Although She had never been there before and no one had given Her directions or asked Her to go there, Amma went directly to the Krishna devotee's house. She walked the entire distance of seven or eight kilometers. Entering the prayer room, Amma picked up from the altar a vessel containing sweet pudding and began to eat a little bit.

The man was dumbfounded when he saw Amma doing this. It was his daily custom to cook sweet pudding and place it in his prayer room as an offering to Lord Krishna. Now he saw that Amma had come and accepted the offering. From that day onward, he became a strong devotee of Amma.

Later, he said that on that particular day, when he placed the sweet pudding on his altar before Krishna's picture, he told himself that only if Amma came and accepted his offering to Krishna would he believe She was Lord Krishna.

On another occasion, this same devotee went to a pond to bathe and accidentally ventured into an area that was too deep for him. He did not know how to swim, and he began to drown. By Amma's grace, he was able to remember Her while struggling for his life. He began to shout, "Amma! Amma!" Suddenly he saw Amma standing above the water just in front of him. Amma showed him how to use his hands and legs to keep afloat and get out of the water. Even though he didn't believe he would be able to follow Amma's instructions, he felt an external force moving his limbs in order to keep him afloat. In this way his life was saved. He would often relate these profound experiences to others.

This devotee had adopted an orphan boy as his son. Amma allowed the boy to put up a small tea shop on the ashram property.

There were no restaurants or hotels near the ashram in those days. As hundreds of devotees visited his tea shop on the way to see Amma, his business was booming. He was making a lot of money, and even giving a major portion of the profit to his adopted father. The devotee did not even have to work because of the money he received from his adopted son's earnings. They were both very happy with the situation.

Some years passed, and more and more people started to visit Amma. There was often a big crowd at the ashram, and there were not enough facilities to accommodate the increasing number of devotees. Amma wanted to build more rooms for them as well as a prayer hall and a dining hall. Amma explained the situation to the boy and asked him to relocate his tea shop so that the ashram property, which he was using for his tea shop, could be used to build more facilities for the devotees. The boy told his adopted father what Amma had said. On hearing this news, the man became very upset, saying, "Why should Amma ask my son to move his shop?" Because they were both making so much money from the tea shop, he did not like hearing that Amma wanted it moved.

It is worth mentioning that most of the people, especially those who lived in the nearby villages in those days, thought differently about Amma than people do today. The villagers knew that Amma would manifest Devi Bhava and Krishna Bhava[11] during certain

---

[11] Amma regularly gives a special darshan where She appears in the mood and dress of Devi. At that time, She is completely identified with God in the form of the Divine Mother. Earlier, She used to give darshan in Krishna Bhava as well. About these special bhavas (moods), Amma once said, "All the deities of the Hindu pantheon, which represent the numberless aspects of the One Supreme Being, exist within us. One possessing

days each week. They thought it was only during those days that Amma could become God, Devi, or Krishna. They thought that Amma was being visited by external divine forces only on those particular days, and on other days Amma was like any other ordinary human being. Such was their faith. So when this devotee heard that Amma had asked his son to move the shop, his first question was, "When did Amma say that?" He was wondering whether it was during Devi Bhava or during the "ordinary time." He went on to say, "I have to ask Devi about this."

During Devi Bhava or Krishna Bhava, people would call Amma either Amma or Krishna. During other times they used to refer to Her as "*kunju*," which means "child," or "*mol*," which means "daughter," or by Her given name, Sudhamani. Some of the brahmacharis, also thinking that Amma and Devi were separate but still considering Amma as their Guru, would call Her Amma at ordinary times and Devi Amma during Devi Bhava. Sometimes we would come to see Amma during the day, and She wouldn't pay any attention to us — She would be talking to another devotee or be immersed in meditation. When this happened, we would go to Amma during Devi Bhava and complain, "Devi Amma, Amma didn't even look at me today. Please tell Her to pay more attention to me in the future." Amma (in Devi Bhava) would say, "Don't worry, I'll talk to Amma." Because our attitude was that Amma and Devi were separate, Amma acted as if that were true.

Divine Power can manifest any of them by his mere will for the good of the world. Here is a crazy girl who puts on the garb of Krishna and after some time that of Devi, but it is within this crazy girl that both exist. "Why decorate an elephant? Why does a policeman wear a uniform and a cap? All these external aids are meant to create a certain impression. In a like manner, Amma dons the garb of Krishna and Devi in order to give strength to the devotional attitude of the people coming for darshan."

So this devotee came during Devi Bhava darshan and said to Amma, "Devi, is it true that Kunju told my son to remove his shop from the ashram property?"

Amma explained, "See, Kunju asked your son to move the shop because the ashram is badly in need of some land. Many of the devotees do not even have a place to rest. Some of them are old and sick, and they need proper accommodations."

Upon hearing Amma's words, the devotee forgot he was talking to Devi at the time. He became so upset that he left the ashram immediately and never came back to see Amma. Because his devotion was not based on knowledge, he could not make use of all the beautiful experiences he had had with Amma. When Amma said something he did not like, all his faith and devotion disappeared in an instant.

He thought Amma was just an agent for him to fulfill his desires. Amma calls this type of devotion "business bhakti." Such devotion can never be steady. When we have business bhakti, our love and devotion for God will increase whenever God answers our prayers. When we think our prayers have gone unanswered, our love and devotion will decrease.

True devotion is not affected by anything that happens in life. If we read Amma's life story, we can see that Amma always had steady devotion to God, no matter what experiences She had to undergo. In Her early life, Amma received only abuse and ill treatment from Her family members, Her neighbors, and the nearby villagers, but Her devotion never wavered because of these adverse experiences. Whenever She experienced adversity, Amma thought, "God is giving me an opportunity to develop the qualities of endurance and forbearance." This is the attitude of a true devotee.

If we are able to develop such an attitude, there will never be a reason to be angry with God, even if things are going against our wishes. Instead, we will be able to accept unpleasant experiences as opportunities to cultivate spiritual qualities such as patience, acceptance, and equanimity.

When Amma's brahmacharis commit mistakes, She is very strict with them because they have come to Amma with the sole aim of realizing God. Thus, She wants the brahmacharis to perform each and every action with that goal in mind. Once, when a brahmachari in the ashram made a mistake, Amma told him, "I am not going to talk to you." Hearing this, he was very upset; that is the worst punishment one can receive from Amma. Even if Amma scolds us, it may not affect us much, but if Amma won't talk to us, it is very painful for us. Every morning this brahmachari would go and try to apologize to Amma, but Amma refused to listen. More than a week passed in this way. Finally, it became too much for him. One day, after Her morning darshan, he followed Amma closely on the way to Her room. Before the door was closed, he sneaked into the room without Amma noticing. When Amma closed the door, She found the brahmachari inside the room.

Without saying a word, Amma took him by the arm and showed him the door. The brahmachari waited outside for a while and then came down the stairs. I ran into him as he was leaving. He told me what had just happened. Then he added, "But I am not unhappy. Actually, I am very happy now."

"Amma still hasn't spoken to you, how can you be happy?" I asked him.

"At least Amma touched me," he replied. "Even though She showed me the door, She was holding my arm. That is enough for me."

Later, when I told Amma what the brahmachari had told me, She was so happy to hear about his attitude. The next day, Amma started speaking to him again. She explained to him that She could never really be angry with anyone, and that Her treatment toward him had just been an act She put on to make him aware of his mistake.

When we have true devotion, we will never find fault with God or the Guru. In order to ensure that our devotion never wavers or fades away, it should be built on a solid foundation of knowledge. Such steadfast devotion will definitely accelerate our spiritual growth and strengthen our bond with God or the Guru. ❖

CHAPTER 22

The Vision of the Scriptures

It is helpful to gain a basic knowledge of the scriptures of Sanatana Dharma, especially for a spiritual seeker. The scriptures give us a clear vision of the goal of human life and the means to achieve that goal. Having some knowledge of the scriptures will also help us to understand Mahatmas to some extent.

Even if we are not able to study the scriptures, by keenly observing a Satguru's actions and words and implicitly following their instructions, we will be able to reach the spiritual goal. Because Mahatmas are established in the Supreme Knowledge, whatever they say is equal to the words of the scriptures. That is why Mahatmas like Amma are referred to as "the living scriptures."

When we decided to have an emblem for Amma's ashram, the brahmacharis were discussing which quotation we should select. Finally, we couldn't come to any conclusion, so we went to Amma and asked Her, "Amma, we want your help. Please give us a quotation we can put beneath the ashram emblem." Initially She said, "Just select any quotation you like." We tried, but we could not reach a consensus. One day we were casually talking with Amma, and unexpectedly She said, "Children, liberation can be gained through renunciation." Of course, it was not in Sanskrit; She spoke these words in Malayalam. Immediately one of the brahmacharis recalled a phrase from one of the Upanishads with a very similar meaning: "*tyagenaike amrtatvamanasuhu.*" Amma had never read any scriptures, but She gave a quotation with the same meaning as this scriptural statement. With Amma's permission, we incorporated this scriptural quote into the ashram emblem.

The most ancient of all scriptures, the Vedas were not composed by any human author but were "revealed" to the ancient rishis, or seers. The mantras composing the Vedas were already there in nature in the form of subtle vibrations; the rishis attained such a deep state of absorption that they were able to perceive these mantras.

The ideas contained in the Vedas are classified into two parts. The *Karma Kanda* (Ritual Portion) describes many rituals for the fulfillment of specific desires. Suppose you want to have a child; there is a ritual for that. If you want to go to heaven, there is another ritual. Even thousands of years ago, people were performing these rituals to effectively fulfill their desires. To achieve any specific desire, a lot of specific observances are required. One has to get up from the bed facing a certain direction, chant certain mantras before, during and after taking a bath, before eating, etc. Then while performing the ritual itself, there are many steps to be followed, each accompanied by specific mantras and prayers. Some of these rituals last for several days. While these mantras are effective in achieving the particular desire, they also have a subtle positive effect on the person chanting them. When a person performs a few such rituals, the mind becomes more and more pure and attuned to God. Under this positive influence, there is even a possibility that this person will become a spiritual seeker. The Karma Kanda helps ordinary people fulfill ordinary desires, and simultaneously kindles within them an interest in spirituality.

The second portion of the Vedas is called the *Jnana Kanda* (Knowledge Portion). This part of the Vedas focuses exclusively on Brahman, the Ultimate Truth. Compared to the ritual portion, which has thousands of pages, the Jnana Kanda is very small. This shows that desires are many, but the Truth, which is the basis of all else, is only One.

Even though Amma is a Self-realized Master, most people don't ask for any spiritual knowledge. Instead, we go to Amma with our day-to-day problems and concerns. Suppose I didn't get straight A's in my exams — I got one B plus. For me, that's very important because I wanted to be first in my class. In reality, my life is not going to suffer because I came in second. But if I share my sorrow with Amma, She will definitely express Her sympathy and offer me encouragement and blessings for the future.

Or sometimes, people come to Amma and tell Her that their cow is not yielding enough milk and ask if She could please bless the cow so it will give more milk. Or someone might say, "There is no water in my well, Amma; please help me." She will give them some *vibhuti* (sacred ash) and tell them to put it in the cow's food or into the well. Even though these things are very insignificant from the point of view of a God-realized soul, Amma knows that these problems are very real for the people in these situations, and She takes a great deal of care in listening to such problems and giving solutions.

When we first met Amma, imagine if She had told us, "Everything you desire is *mithya* (impermanent). Only God is permanent. Ask only for God-realization — I can help you attain That." Most of us would have run for the door. We all have many desires, and we want those desires to be fulfilled. As we keep coming to Amma to get our desires fulfilled, we are also affected in a subtle way by Amma's unconditional love and spiritual energy. Slowly, we will start turning toward spirituality. In this way, we can see that Amma is indeed the living scriptures — She functions exactly like the Vedas. For those who want only knowledge of the Supreme Truth, She will help them attain That. For those who have worldly desires, She will help them attain those (provided they are righteous aims or goals).

Amma says that in order to get the maximum benefit from the scriptures, we must perform the duties prescribed by them. It is not enough if we just read the scriptures like we read the newspaper. We must be able to discharge the duties and responsibilities the scriptures have given us. Fulfilling our duties is not always pleasant because we all have our own likes and dislikes. Still the scriptures insist that we do our duties and fulfill our responsibilities. What is the benefit of following these instructions? When we faithfully perform the duties enjoined by the scriptures or given by the Guru, slowly we are able to transcend our likes and dislikes.

The Vedas tell us, "*Satyam vada,*" which means, "Speak the truth." We may not always want to speak the truth, but if we want to follow the teachings of the Vedas, we will try to speak the truth even though we don't always feel like it. In this way we will be able to overcome our tendency toward telling lies when it is convenient for us.

We always avoid things that we don't like or think we will not like. But if we don't have the proper understanding, we will end up avoiding things that may be useful or good for us. Following the scriptural instructions will always be for our benefit.

The scriptures have classified all possible actions into five major types, and given us different instructions regarding each type.

The first type of action is called *kamya karma*, or the actions we perform to fulfill our many desires. The scriptures do not prohibit this type of action, but remind us that acting in this way will not lead us to the ultimate goal of Self-realization. (The rituals outlined in the Karma Kanda fall under the category of kamya karma.)

Regarding kamya karma, Amma says there is nothing wrong in performing actions to fulfill our desires — as long as those actions are righteous — but that we should understand that these desires will not give us permanent happiness and that it may not be possible to achieve everything we desire.

The second type of action is called *nitya karma*. Nitya karma applies to our daily activities, and to the actions or observances that we are supposed to do every day. Even for routine actions such as brushing our teeth, taking a bath, and eating, specific mantras are prescribed that will help us to remember that it is not by our power that we are performing actions but by the power of Brahman, which sustains the whole universe. Thinking in this way will also help us to remember the spiritual goal of life. For those who have a Guru, following the Guru's instructions for daily practices is their nitya karma. Amma suggests we chant our mantra and meditate every day. People with a devotional attitude can also chant the 108 Names or the 1000 Names of the Divine Mother (or the God or Goddess of their preference.)

Actions to be performed on special occasions are called *naimithika karma*. There is a special naming ceremony when a newborn baby is given a name, a special ritual performed during the first feeding of solid food, a ritual on the baby's first birthday, etc. Every year we are to offer oblations to the departed souls, to our ancestors. And every year Brahmins have a ceremony wherein they discard the old sacred thread and put on a new one. There are many such rituals to be performed on specific occasions; these are just a few examples.

Amma asks us to help and serve others whenever we get an opportunity. She even says that if we do not have any opportunity to serve, we should create one. Of course, we may not get opportunities to serve others every day, but if we make an effort, we can definitely find ways to help others. We can visit hospitals, homes for the elderly or orphanages or other such establishments at regular intervals and help in whatever way is needed.

In addition, many people do not have an opportunity to chant archana in a group setting on a daily basis. In that case, they can get together with other devotees once a week or once a month and participate in group archana, meditation, and bhajans. This form of satsang, along with selfless service, can be taken as the naimithika karma of Amma's children.

Then there are some acts (*nishiddha karma*) that should never be done. The scriptures tell us not to lie, not to steal, not to harm or hate others, and not to cheat or speak ill of others. And yet, if we analyze our life, we will find that we are performing some of these prohibited actions at least occasionally. That means we are strengthening these negative tendencies and instead of gaining the good, positive vibrations we would get from performing the duties the scriptures have given us, we are gaining only negative vibrations. These negativities, in turn, become an obstacle in our spiritual practices.

Amma says very clearly that when we have bad intentions toward another person, we should remember that Amma is in that person as well. Or when we feel angry with a person, we should try to think of something good that person did for us in the past.

Amma is making these suggestions in order to steer us away from nishiddha karma, or actions prohibited by the scriptures.

Finally, there are the remedial actions we can perform to either nullify or reduce the negative results we are destined to experience because of the harmful actions we have performed intentionally. These actions are called *prayaschitta karma*.

The scriptures describe different types of prayaschitta karma, depending on the type and degree of the harmful action. These include certain rituals and observances, as well as giving particular things in charity. It is said that the effects of harmful actions we have done can also be reduced or eliminated by performing tapas under the guidance of a Guru, or by the grace of God.

There are many cases of devotees who found that their astrological chart predicted some tragedy would befall them during a certain period of their life. Of course this incident was part of their destiny because of some negative action they had committed in the past, either in the present life or a previous one. In such cases Amma would often give a certain prescription such as fasting or observing a vow of silence on a particular day every week for a number of months or years. When the devotee faithfully performed the prayaschitta karma as Amma instructed, the disaster would be averted.

The scriptures also ask us to perform the *panchamahayagna* (five great sacrifices). When we hear the word sacrifice, we may think it means killing an animal as an offering to God. Actually, in Sanatana Dharma, sacrifice has nothing to do with killing. In this context, sacrifice means sharing. We sacrifice our own comforts and selfish desires in order to develop the spirit of sharing with one and all: human beings as well as animals and plants. This will help to maintain the harmony in nature and in the world.

Everybody kills living beings, knowingly or unknowingly. When we walk, we may be inadvertently killing insects or some other small living beings. Likewise, there are many insects living in the bark of firewood. When we use firewood for cooking or heating our home, many insects will die. When a mosquito lands on us, we kill it. After driving on a highway, our windshield will be covered with dead insects. We may even hit a deer or run over some other animal. Unintentionally we have killed so many creatures in our life. Thus, the scriptures give us five different types of *yagnas* (sacrifices) we can perform to nullify the negative effects of the harmful actions we have performed inadvertently and to express our gratitude to God, the five elements, other human beings, animals, and our ancestors. Our life is made possible only through the help we receive from these five sources.

The first yagna enjoined by the scriptures is the *Brahma yagna*, which is to learn (through study of the scriptures) about Brahman, or God, and to teach others what we have learned. The Brahma yagna is suggested as an expression of gratitude to Brahman or God. Since Brahman is the source of everything, we owe our very existence to Brahman. It is not for God's sake that we perform this yagna — recollecting our dependence on God can help us to cultivate humility, and sharing the moral and spiritual values outlined in the scriptures helps to maintain harmony in society. Actually, God doesn't want or need our worship; He is full and perfect. Amma says that the sun doesn't need the help of a candle. The sun gives light to the whole world; of what use is a candle to the sun? Likewise, God doesn't need our worship. It is only for our own benefit that we are worshipping.

In olden times, only the Brahmins (priestly class) were authorized to perform this yagna because only the Brahmins were supposed to study the scriptures, but many of Amma's children are performing this yagna every day. When we meet our friends, we usually talk about Amma. Since Amma is one with God, when we talk about Amma we are actually talking about God.

The next yagna the scriptures ask us to perform is the *pitr yagna*, or the rituals we perform for our departed ancestors. In India, the most common way of performing this yagna is to offer one ball of rice (or any other staple food) to crows with the resolve that our departed ancestors will be benefited by our prayers and nourished by the food we have offered. One may feel it is foolish to offer food for a dead person, as he or she cannot eat it. According to the Vedas, departed spirits exist in an intermediary plane called *pitr loka* (world of the departed) until they take a new body. While in this intermediary plane, they feel hunger and thirst but cannot consume anything on their own. The subtle vibrations of the food we offer to them is the food for their subtle body. Our prayers augment their spiritual progress and help them to attain a higher birth.

The pitr yagna with all the rituals described in the Vedas generally is performed only once a year. In some highly orthodox families, they do this ritual every month, but it is enough to do it once a year. When Amma conducts the Devi Puja or Atma Puja, She asks us to pray for the peace of our departed ancestors. So in that way, we are performing this yagna as well.

The third yagna is the *deva yagna*. In the tradition of Sanatana Dharma, there are deities associated with each and every element and aspect of creation, such as earth, air, speech, action, mind, intelligence, etc. Just as the same electricity powers different appliances, all these deities are considered different aspects of one God. Even though God is only one, in order to meet our various day-to-day requirements, that power is made available to our mind through various names and forms. Each one has a different application and expression.

The devas worshipped in the deva yagna are the presiding deities of the natural forces. We get air, water, light and land from nature — all for free. Maybe we have to pay the government for water and electricity, but nature doesn't charge us anything. As we are thus indebted to these natural forces, we are supposed to express our gratitude to the presiding deities through the deva yagna.

At the start of the Devi Puja, Amma performs the deva yagna on our behalf. Incorporating all five elements, She takes the pot containing pure water, sanctifies it with sacred ash (representing earth), and waves the burning camphor (representing fire) while ringing a bell (the sound representing space). Then She breathes (representing air) into the water transmitting Her *prana shakti* (vital force).

The fourth yagna is called *bhuta yagna*. This is the service we render to other living beings. In India, generally cows are especially cared for because the cow is considered a sacred animal. Likewise, the *tulasi* (basil) plant is considered sacred and devoted householders pay their respects to it daily. In the West, in many houses, there are one or two pet cats or a dog. Of course, we cannot help every animal. Whatever help we can render to any animal or plant we come into contact with is enough. The scriptures say that even if you don't have an animal in your house, it is enough to just feed other animals such as birds, deer, cattle, or squirrels, or to water a plant or care for a tree. Many different animals play a role in making our life possible. Taking care of one or two abandoned or wounded animals or birds, or working for the protection of an endangered species are all various ways we can show our gratitude and repay our debt to other living beings. Amma's international GreenFriends initiative provides an opportunity for Her children to perform the bhuta yagna.

Finally there is the *nara yagna*, or service to our fellow human beings. Whenever we see someone needing help, we should help them without expecting anything in return. If you come across an old person who is having a difficult time crossing the road, just help them cross the road. The spirit of yagna is sacrifice, or selflessness. Whatever action is done without expecting anything is a yagna. If I am helping a person and I am not expecting any reward for my help, it becomes a real sacrifice — it becomes a yagna.

Many of Amma's children help support Her humanitarian activities in one way or another. When we donate money or offer other assistance to Amma's charities, such as volunteering in Her house-building project in India (Amrita Kuteeram) or in Her project for feeding the poor (in the United States, called Mother's Kitchen) or any of the other numerous projects Amma has initiated to alleviate the suffering of the poor and needy, we are performing the nara yagna.

The purpose of all these activities is not simply to do as the scriptures tell us; all these yagnas are for our own benefit. When we perform these duties sincerely, we become more expansive—we grow spiritually. If we find ourselves performing these actions out of a sense of obligation, the same way we go to our job simply because we have to, we won't receive the maximum benefit. Amma gives a good example to illustrate this point. Often, if a person donates something to a temple or any charitable or spiritual organization, he or she will want others to know who made the donation. Amma made a joke that if somebody donates even a fluorescent tube light, they will write "donated by so and so" on the tube and half the light we would have received is blocked by their painted declaration. This kind of donation is made out of a motivation to help, of course, but it is also done for name and fame. In such cases, the person donates something to the temple thinking it is an act of worship, but they don't understand the true spirit of worship. When we donate money to a charitable or humanitarian cause, we should be able to think that the money was given to us by God, and we are just giving it back to Him.

Whatever the Master advises or instructs us to do will be in perfect accordance with the scriptures. We have seen that Amma has given clear instructions on the five types of actions and the five great sacrifices that are perfectly in line with the scriptural injunctions. We should not worry that we cannot remember all five types of actions, or that we will not be able to memorize the five great sacrifices. The scriptures say that following a Master's instructions with sincerity will make up for any lapses in following the scriptural instructions.

Of course, scriptural knowledge by itself is not enough. Amma says the vision of the scriptures and the strength of spiritual practice are both needed for us to eliminate our negativities and to hold firmly on to God. ❖

CHAPTER 23

Spirituality in Action

Worship is not something to be done just at certain times or on certain days. Likewise, *sadhana* (spiritual practice) does not just mean meditation and chanting. As Amma puts it, each and every action in our life should become a sadhana. Otherwise, our spiritual practice will become confined only to the morning meditation or the evening prayers. In Amma's case, even the games She played with Her friends when She was very young were a sadhana. When She was five or six years old, Amma would play in the backwaters with Her friends. They often played a game in which each child would go underwater to see who was able to hold their breath for the longest time. Whoever was able to remain underwater the longest would win. Amma would go under water making the firm resolve that only after chanting Her mantra a certain number of times — maybe 100 times or 150 times — would She come up to the surface. Sometimes She would be under water for more than two minutes. The other children would even become frightened thinking that Amma might have drowned. To all the onlookers, it would seem that Amma was just trying to win the game. But actually through playing that game, She was doing Her spiritual practice.

They also used to play hide and seek. Sometimes Amma would climb to the top of a tree so the others wouldn't be able to see Her. Then She would imagine Herself to be Lord Krishna and that all Her friends were Krishna's childhood friends, the *gopis* (milkmaids) and *gopas* (cowherd boys). Through this game also, She was able to remember God.

In the village where Amma grew up, no one had running water inside their home. Everyone had to rely on the few public water taps. And at that time, there was not even a pump with which to draw out the water. Instead, one had to rely on a windmill attached to the well. When the wind was blowing, the wheel would turn and one could get water from the tap. But if the wind was not blowing, one had no choice but to wait. When this happened, the villagers standing in line at the well would become very restless and impatient, walking to and fro and even cursing aloud. Only Amma, who was there to carry water for Her entire household, would remain calm. She used this time as an opportunity to remember God, closing Her eyes and silently chanting Her mantra. Because of Her attitude, everything She did became a spiritual practice.

Of course, Amma did not really need to do any sadhana, as She was born enlightened. It was only to serve as an example to others that She acted in this way. If we practice in this way, instead of just doing one or two hours of sadhana each day, most of our daily activities can be converted into sadhana.

There is a devotee who often comes to Amritapuri. Whenever he comes, he volunteers to help in cleaning the ashram grounds. After Amma gives darshan to thousands of visitors, the ground is often strewn with the plastic wrappers from the candies which Amma gives as prasad. This devotee spends hours picking up each wrapper by hand. Seeing this, another devotee offered him a broom, saying, "Why don't you use a broom? It will be so much quicker that way." The first devotee smiled and politely declined the offer. "When I see these wrappers on the ground, I don't see them as waste. These wrappers are Amma's prasad — Amma has held each one of these wrappers in Her hand. When I think in this way, I can't sweep them away with a broom. I don't mind spending any number of hours picking them up. When I pick them up off the ground, I remember that each one has been touched and blessed by Amma."

Amma says that whatever we say, whatever we do, whatever we think — if it is done in the right way, it is spirituality.

When we compare our life span with the life span of the universe, we see that our life is very short. We should not be complacent thinking that we have 60 or 80 years to do sadhana and reach our goal. In fact, we don't have that much time. Even out of this 60 or 80 years, almost one third of our life is spent sleeping. So out of 80 years we are sleeping for nearly 27 years, and more than 25 years is spent in childhood play and youthful pursuits. Most people work eight hours a day for 40 years—that is 13 more years when we can't really perform any spiritual practices. Then, at the end of our life, we become weak and unable to perform long hours of sadhana — so that is another 10 years gone. That means that even if we live for 80 years, we really only have five years when we can perform spiritual practices, and even during that time there will be so many problems and distractions. That is why it is so important that we learn to convert all of our actions into sadhana. Whether we are caring for a spouse or children or working, we should try to develop an attitude through which we will be able to perform all these actions as sadhana. Even our troubles in life can become sadhana, if through those difficulties we are able to remember God. That's why Amma says all the difficulties in Her life were like Gurus for Her.

The easiest way to convert our actions into sadhana is to perform our actions in the spirit of worship. This means that we put forth our best effort and surrender the results of our actions at the feet of the Lord. When we act with this understanding, we know that we have done our best and that it is up to God to determine the result.

The scriptures say that if whatever we do is surrendered at the feet of the Lord, we will not be karmically bound by the result of the action. Otherwise, we will have to experience the reaction or result. For instance, if we harm someone or steal something, naturally the result is that we will go to jail. If we happen to escape the punishment in this life, it will definitely come to us in a future birth. That is the reason we see so many people suffering in the world. They might not have done anything wrong in their present life, yet so many unfortunate things will befall them. This is because of actions they have performed in previous births. They are simply experiencing the results of their own actions.

The present life is a continuation of our past lives. The results of our past actions that we have not yet experienced will have to be experienced one day, either now or in the future. For example, some people are born into very difficult circumstances. A person born into such a painful situation must have done some harmful action in a previous life. Otherwise, we would have to say that God is cruel. Of course, this does not mean that people who are having a lot of difficulty in their life should feel guilty about having done something harmful in a previous life. We have all lived many lives on this earth, we have all performed hurtful actions, and we are all suffering as a result. Until we realize our True Self, we will not be infallible.

In truth, God is impartial. Whatever action we do comes back to us as a reaction. This is the Law of Karma. When we are doing an action with the attitude, "I am doing," naturally, the result—good or bad—must come to us. It will not go to our neighbor. Each of us has a karmic debt that must be paid. Of course, Mahatmas like Amma can alleviate our suffering by removing or reducing the problem or by giving us the strength to endure it. The important thing for us is to do our best not to create any more negative prarabdha. That is why Amma always reminds us to be ever so careful in our every thought, word, and deed — it is our thoughts, words, and actions in the present that determine our experiences in the future. If you are suffering a great deal in this life, try to think that you are exhausting a lot of your remaining prarabdha.

The life of every living being is a constant struggle to reduce pain and increase happiness. In our effort to gain personal happiness, sometimes we cause sorrow and pain for others, either inadvertently or intentionally. Every living being is surrounded by an aura, a subtle layer on which is recorded all of our thoughts, words, and actions. We bring this aura with us when are born, and it will accompany us after death. When we intentionally cause sorrow or pain for others, it will be recorded in our aura, and in due course of time, bring misery and suffering to us. On the other hand, if we bring joy and peace to others, these actions will invariably bring more blessings and happiness into our life. Once again, this is the Law of Karma. It is because of this law that our life passes like a pendulum, oscillating between pain and pleasure.

A spiritual aspirant who wants to break free from the cycle of birth and death must learn to perform every action as an offering to the Lord. For a spiritual aspirant, even the result of a good action will become bondage if he or she is attached to the result. It is like being bound by a golden chain. Whether we are bound by a golden chain or an iron chain, it's still bondage. Even if we have done only good actions, as long as we are attached to the results, we will have to take another birth just to experience those good results. Good and bad actions alike will always bind us as long as they are performed with a sense of ego, or "I am doing." If we want to get rid of this bondage, we must perform every action with a spirit of worship and surrender.

Of course, we can only offer good actions to the Lord. We cannot commit murder or some other crime, thinking that we are offering the action to God and we can escape the consequences of our actions. If we commit any bad action, we will definitely experience the result.

When we offer something to God without any expectation, it is real worship. If we expect something in return, it is not true worship. Instead it is like a business transaction — we are bargaining. When we perform all our actions as worship of God, we accept the results of our actions as God's gift to us. We won't be upset with the result of our action, whatever it may be — we will be able to accept it as given by God. Generally, if our action does not produce the intended result, we get upset or depressed. However, if we have the attitude of surrender and acceptance and the result is not as we expected, we won't be upset. The proper attitude is, "Okay, Lord, You gave me the power and the energy to do this action. Now I have done the action, and I am offering it at Your feet. I am not demanding anything. Whatever is Your will, let me accept it." Thinking thus, we will be able to accept the ups and downs of life with equanimity.

In the *Bhagavad Gita*, Lord Krishna declares,

karmaṇy evādhikāras te mā phaleṣu kadācana

You have mastery only over your actions,
Not over their fruits (results). (2.47)

This does not mean that the Lord wants us to work without expecting remuneration. Actually, here Krishna is explaining one of the basic laws of nature, as impersonal as Newton's laws of motion. He simply states that we do not have complete control over all factors affecting the outcome of our action.

Therefore, the results will not always be as we think they should be. The universal intelligence, which is otherwise called God, determines the result.

Amma gives a beautiful example for this. Suppose we take a handful of seeds and, holding them in our palm, fervently pray to God to make them sprout. Even though God is omnipotent, and even if our prayers are sincere, the seeds are not going to sprout as long as they remain in our hands. In order that they sprout, we have to plant the seeds beneath good, fertile soil. Only then is there a chance that they will sprout. However, is there any guarantee that all of those seeds will become plants or that each plant will give the same yield? The results are unpredictable because they depend on many factors beyond our control. We have the right to plant the seeds; that is all. When the Lord says we should concentrate on the action and leave the results to God, it is practical advice.

Surrender is a positive way of living; it is not pessimism or fatalism. When we cultivate an attitude of surrender and acceptance, we can conserve our energy. At present, when something goes wrong in our life, we tend to brood over it. In this way, we are wasting so much energy and time. If we accept whatever comes with a positive attitude, thinking that this is Amma's will or God's will, we can use our time and energy creatively.

As Amma's children, it will be easy for us to cultivate an attitude of surrender and acceptance. If we have any doubt or concern, we can always get Amma's help and guidance. Without a living Master, it is more difficult to maintain this kind of attitude as it is not possible for us to get guidance directly from God. Of course, God is always there for us, but we are not always receptive enough to receive God's guidance. In such a situation, a living Master who has come down to our level is a great blessing for us.

There are reasons why the scriptures say that we shouldn't be too concerned about the results of our actions. One reason is that we might lose our inspiration and enthusiasm. If we focus too much on the result, we become tense and sometimes even lose the strength to continue putting forth effort.

After graduating from college, I applied for a job in a pharmaceutical company and was called for an interview. The officer who was interviewing me asked questions that were very easy for me to answer. I was wondering why this man was asking me all these simple questions. I had been expecting challenging questions because it was an attractive job. However, all the questions were straightforward, so I thought maybe he had already decided to hire one of the other candidates and interviewing me was just a formality. The thought that I might not get the job after all created some disturbances in my mind.

Suddenly the interviewer gave me an unexpected question: On which side of the frog is its heart located? Is it on the right side or the left side? Such a simple question; I had dissected a frog many times in zoology classes and had traced its vascular system so I knew very well on which side its heart was. But in that moment my mind was divided, worrying that someone else might have gotten the job. I was thinking about what my next plan should be in case I didn't get the job. When the interviewer asked, I answered incorrectly, "It is on the left side." Needless to say, I did not get the job.

Why couldn't I answer such a simple question? I couldn't respond correctly because I was overly concerned about the result of the interview. It often happens to us that we perform a task poorly because we are more focused on the result than on the task at hand. That is why Amma always tells us to concentrate more on the present action instead of thinking about the outcome. If we are more careful and attentive in our actions, the future will take care of itself.

Whenever we find ourselves in circumstances beyond our control, we should try to take the situation as given by God and try to be sincere in our responsibilities. In this way we will be worshipping God.

For example, we have to take proper care of our children. This is our duty. If the children don't reciprocate our love, we shouldn't resent them. We should try to be interested only in performing our duty, not in the result of the action. This is the proper spirit of worship.

Suppose I want to live with Amma in Her ashram in India but I am not able to because I have so many responsibilities with regard to my family. There are many such people. To them, Amma says, "Whatever duty you have toward your family, do it as worship, thinking that your family was given by Amma, and that Amma has given you the responsibility to take care of them. This is as good as worshipping Amma."

Many years ago, when I was working in a bank, I wanted to leave my job and be in the ashram full time, but I was not able to because I had some financial commitments to my family. I thought that I was wasting my time by working in the bank, but Amma told me, "This should not be your attitude. You must try to love your job. When the customers are coming to you, think that I am sending them to you. By serving them sincerely, you are worshipping Amma, and you will not be wasting your time."

Whenever you find yourself in an unpleasant situation from which you cannot escape, try not to be upset about your circumstances. Think that this has been given to you by Amma for the time being, and try to respond to the situation with sincerity and dedication. Try to remember that by putting us in different situations and circumstances, Amma is molding us into a perfect instrument to receive Her grace. Performing our actions with a spirit of worship and surrender will ultimately eliminate our ego and help us realize our innate divinity — our oneness with the Ultimate Truth. ❖

CHAPTER 24

Recognizing a Mahatma

Once there was a world famous lion trainer. She could perform tricks with the most ferocious of felines that no other circus performer had ever attempted. An awestruck audience always packed the stadium wherever she traveled and marveled at her feats of daring.

First, she would demonstrate the fierce nature of the lion, beckoning him to roar and appear as if he was going to pounce. Then she would perform a series of tricks with the lion to show that she was not at all afraid of the beast. The culmination of her act was to place a piece of sugar candy on her tongue and allow the lion to lick it off. Whenever she performed this stunt, the crowd went wild.

At one performance, the Mullah Nasruddin happened to be in the crowd. The lion tamer began her act, and the crowd grew excited, applauding each time she put the ferocious lions through their paces. Finally, she came to the finale. In front of the largest and most ferocious of the lions, she knelt down and put a sugar cube on her tongue. The lion gently removed the sugar cube. The crowd roared with appreciation for her act of daring. However, the voice of the Mullah could be heard above the crowd, yelling, "That's nothing! Anybody could do that!" Hearing his comments, the lion tamer walked out of the cage up to where the Mullah was standing.

She challenged the Mullah, saying, "You say anybody could do it. Can you do it?"

The Mullah retorted, "If the lion could, anyone could." The Mullah was missing the obvious — he was comparing himself to the lion rather than the lion trainer, thinking it did not take much courage at all on the lion's part to do what he had done.

This story shows us that two people can look at the same act and see very different things. It all depends on our perspective. This is why some people can receive Amma's darshan and miss Her greatness, while many others feel inspired and transformed.

Many years ago, two seekers came to the ashram to meet Amma. They had visited many ashrams without finding a Guru who could impress and inspire them. They heard that Amma was a Realized Master, and they decided to come and see for themselves.

At that time, Amma used to have some free time during the day. Thus, She was able to do many things that She no longer has the time for: She would spend many hours absorbed in samadhi each day, and She would often come and help in the kitchen to cook food for the brahmacharis and devotees. She would also spend some time playing with the neighborhood children. When these two newcomers arrived, they saw Amma running back and forth, shouting and laughing as She played a local game with the children.

A few brahmacharis and I were standing off to the side enjoying Amma's *lila* (divine play). The newcomers approached me and asked me a few questions about myself. I told them I was working in a nearby bank but staying at the ashram. The men asked me where they could find the Guru of the ashram. "She's right there," I said, pointing to Amma.

"You mean that girl playing with the children?" the men asked me incredulously. At that time, Amma was in Her mid-twenties, and when She was playing with children She could look even younger.

"Yes, yes," I assured them. "She is our Guru." I told the men if they waited for a few minutes, they would be able to meet Amma and receive Her darshan.

The men discussed something between themselves for a minute or two and then left without saying another word.

20 years later, the same men returned to the ashram. Having asked about me, they came to my room. "Do you remember us, Swamiji?" they asked. I had to admit that I did not. They reminded me of the brief interaction we had had so long ago and explained that on that first visit they had come with their own preconceived notions about how a Guru should be. Because Amma was not acting the way they expected a Guru would act, they simply left the place, taking Amma to be just an ordinary girl. Over the years they had heard more and more about Amma, and finally they were convinced enough to return to the ashram.

When they went for Amma's darshan, they both burst into tears realizing how foolish they had been. One of the two was wailing uncontrollably for quite some time. Understanding his mistake was too much for him to bear.

There is an old proverb about the holy Ganges River. It points out that while so many walk across India to bathe in its holy waters, some who live on its banks prefer to take a shower in their own house. In the same way, these two men were so close to Amma at a time when they could have had a lot of personal time and attention from Her. Unfortunately, they could not recognize Her greatness at the time.

Another thing Amma used to do often when She had more free time was to help in the construction work and the cleaning of the ashram. In those days, we were living in thatched-roof huts. Every year we had to replace the thatched roofs, which could only survive one season of heavy monsoon rains. The few brahmacharis staying at the ashram at the time had never lived in huts before coming to the ashram and didn't know much about weaving a thatched roof. Amma would always work among us and guide our efforts; we needed a lot of supervision to build the roofs properly.

One day when we were replacing the roofs, two other newcomers came to the ashram. They saw Amma working among us, shouting instructions across the grounds to those who were working farther away. These two newcomers observed Amma for some time. Finally, they left without approaching Her. At that point, Amma turned to some of us and commented, "They came here looking for a Guru. They expected to see the Guru sitting very dignified on a throne with attendants fanning Her and waiting on Her. Instead, they saw the Guru doing manual labor in a stained dress and shouting instructions. Convinced that Amma was just an ordinary village girl, they left. If they had had a real thirst for a Guru, they would have stayed and waited to meet me. However, they will come back when the time is right." Some years later, those two did return. Now they are ardent devotees of Amma.

I recall a joke that reminds us we cannot always draw an accurate conclusion from appearances. There was a professor who was doing research on cockroaches. Finally, he was ready to divulge his findings with a live demonstration. He placed a cockroach on a table and told it to run. The cockroach ran across the tabletop. He caught it before it ran over the edge and, placing it back in its original position, he removed one of its legs. Then he again instructed the roach to run, setting it free on the tabletop. The roach ran. He retrieved the roach and removed one more of its legs. Still the roach was able to run; it continued to run, and then hobble, and then drag itself across the table as he removed its legs one by one. Finally, he plucked off the last leg and again instructed the roach to run. This time, the roach did not move; how could it go anywhere with no legs? Smiling, the professor looked up at the curious audience to proudly announce his revolutionary new finding: "When a cockroach has no legs, it cannot hear." The professor had observed the behavior of the roach and drawn a completely inaccurate conclusion. In the same way, one can observe the behavior of a Mahatma and fail to recognize them for who they are.

When we come to a Mahatma, we should try to be open and receptive without judging his or her external actions. Not everyone who sees Amma can recognize Her as a Mahatma, at least not immediately. Those of us who have been able to recognize at least a little bit of Amma's greatness are blessed indeed. ❖

CHAPTER 25

Sound, Sight, Touch, Thought: A Master's Methods of Initiation

Initiation by a True Master into a particular mantra or spiritual practice can greatly expedite our progress along the spiritual path. Sometimes the initiation produces immediate results. More often, it produces definite results over an extended period of time. One of the most common — nevertheless important — methods of *diksha* (initiation) is by mantra. Many of us have received mantra diksha from Amma. However, Satgurus can initiate us by various other means as well, depending on our receptivity. If we are receptive to it, a Master can initiate us simply by glancing at us — that is called *nayana diksha*, or initiation through the eyes.

A youth came to see Amma for the first time. Amma was in Devi Bhava at the time. He did not go inside the temple to get darshan; he waited outside. After standing there for a few minutes, suddenly, he started to shiver, shake and jump as if he had taken hold of a live electrical wire. All the other devotees kept their distance, thinking he was possessed.

He then started to speak some broken words, as if he was talking to someone only he could see. When Devi Bhava was over, Amma came out of the temple, and this youth was still speaking garbled words. Amma covered his mouth with Her hand and told him not to talk anymore about what he was seeing.

A short while later he regained his normal consciousness. He told us when Amma had looked at him, he had felt a strange power emanating from Her that entered into him. Then he had seen the form of Kali before him. He was trying to explain all these things, but no one was able to make out what he was saying because his words were still broken. This young man was working in an office at that time, and after this incident, he was unable to work for a week. For an entire week, it seemed as though he was in another world—he wrote many devotional songs and philosophical chants during this time. This is an example of the power of nayana diksha.(Later, Amma gave him mantra initiation as well.)

Another method of initiation is *sparsa diksha* (initiation by touch). For some people, the moment Amma touches them, they feel something like a shock going through their body, and they experience an inner transformation. Perhaps Amma is blessing each and every one who comes to Her with this sort of initiation, without their being aware of it. Amma says She is sowing the seeds now; when the season is right, they will sprout and yield results.

There is another type of initiation called *pada diksha*, or initiation through touch of the foot. This type of initiation is very rare. I know of one occasion that Amma gave pada diksha, but it is not at all customary for Her. When this devotee approached Amma for darshan, She just closed Her eyes. No one expected what She did next — She placed Her right foot on the chest of this devotee. I had been with Amma for so many years and had never seen Amma do this. It was the first time I had ever seen Her touch a devotee with Her foot. Immediately the devotee jumped up and began to shiver as if a strong electrical current was passing through him. Another devotee went to hold him, but Amma said, "Don't disturb him; he is in bliss. Let him do what he likes."

He was shaking for nearly 20 minutes. Then he lay down on the ground. Amma said that She had had a strong feeling that She should touch this devotee with Her foot and that he had been praying intensely for a long time for Amma to do that.

Kabir was a great saint in North India who was born into a Muslim family. Kabir had a strong desire to become a disciple of Ramanand, who was a well-known Master at that time, but Kabir was a Muslim, and Ramanand was a Hindu.

At that time there was such a rift between the two religions that the disciples of Ramanand could not swallow the idea of a Muslim being initiated into their midst, nor would the Muslim community allow Kabir to take initiation from a Hindu Guru. However, Kabir was so intent on receiving initiation from Ramanand that finally he thought up a plan.

Kabir knew that every morning before sunrise, Ramanand went to the river for his bath. One morning Kabir went to the bathing ghat before Ramanand arrived and lay down on one of the many steps leading down to the holy river Ganga. As it was still quite dark, Kabir knew that the Guru would not be able to see him lying there and would accidentally step on him. In India, if our foot happens to touch someone, we touch that person and bring our hand to our forehead as a mark of respect. We also might exclaim, "Ram, Ram," or "Krishna, Krishna," just as people say "Oops!" in the United States.

As expected, when Ramanand was coming down the steps, he happened to step on Kabir. The moment he stepped on Kabir, he realized that he had stepped on a human being and he immediately sought forgiveness by invoking the Lord's name. As he shouted, "Ram, Ram!" he was still standing on Kabir. Kabir took this auspicious combination as initiation from Ramanand. He prostrated at Ramanand's feet and left.

Kabir's trick worked. He was so devoted to Ramanand and the Ram mantra he had received from him that eventually he attained Self-realization. His poems in praise of the power of the mantra and the Guru's grace are treasured by people all over India even today.

There is another type of initiation called *smarana diksha*. Smarana means to think or remember. To give smarana diksha, the Guru will simply think of the disciple. Even though the disciple may be far away from the Guru, the disciple will receive the initiation.

Many years ago, a devotee of Amma visited the Himalayas. He wanted to go as high up in the mountains as possible. The journey would take many days on foot. On the way he passed by a hut, and as it was getting dark, he thought he would ask permission to stay there for the night. When the devotee knocked on the door, there was no response. He waited for some time, but no one came to the door. As there was no other hut nearby, he waited for 10 to 15 minutes. Finally, a young man came out of the hut and asked the devotee what he wanted. He replied that he was on a pilgrimage and needed a place to stay for the night. The young man responded, "I am alone; you are welcome." The youth also looked like a spiritual aspirant; there was a glow about his face. It was true — after arranging a bed for the devotee, the young man sat down to meditate.

The devotee was so tired that he went right to sleep, but when he woke up several hours later, he found the young man still meditating. Later that morning, the devotee asked the young man about his spiritual practices. He said he would often do five or six hours of continuous meditation sitting in one pose. The devotee was also surprised to find a small photo of Amma in the hut. Amma was not well known in those places at that time, so he was wondering how Amma's photo might have come to this remote area. He asked the young man whose picture it was without revealing his identity as a devotee of Amma. The young man replied, "A monk happened to visit Amma's ashram in South India. He received Amma's darshan and was very much impressed, so he bought a small picture of Amma. When he came here, he told me about Amma, and I was so drawn to Her, he left the photo here with me."

The young man continued, "That same night, during my meditation, I felt Amma's presence; She whispered a mantra in my ear, and since then I have been chanting that mantra. I consider Amma as my Guru. After this experience, the quality of my meditation really improved." The devotee was very impressed because this young man was doing such intense spiritual practice. When the devotee came back to Amritapuri, he told Amma about this experience. Amma said, "I have many disciples like this sitting in far away corners. I cannot go to them, and they cannot come to me at present, so I guide them in this way."

A brahmachari at Amma's ashram was very sick when Amma was away in Europe. People thought he was going to die. He, too, thought that his life was coming to an end. He was crying and praying, "Amma, you are far away in Europe, but before I die, I must see you in flesh and blood. Please have mercy on me." While in Europe, we received a phone call from one of the brahmacharis in India about the sick brahmachari's prayer. Amma responded, "He is not going to die. Take it for granted he will be okay." The brahmachari who called us from India was also crying, concerned about the condition of the sick brahmachari. He was pleading with Amma, "Please give him your darshan. Even if he died the next day, he would be so happy having received your darshan."

Two days later, a devotee was going from Europe to India. Amma asked this devotee to carry a garland to India that She had worn and give it to the sick brahmachari. After receiving the garland, the brahmachari started getting better, just as Amma had said he would. Amma's blessings reached the brahmachari through the garland. That was the only way She could go to him because the brahmachari had not evolved to such an extent that would allow him to see Amma in a subtle form.

Whether a Satguru uses these various types of initiation with us depends on our receptivity and our level of spiritual growth. If our level of awareness is not subtle enough to receive the initiation, the Master will not work with us in that way. That is why Amma says, "Make use of the mantra that I have given you." As it is, our minds are not subtle. If we sit for meditation for half an hour, we may only be able to concentrate for a few minutes. Even to get that few minutes of concentration is very, very difficult. Until we attain subtlety and concentration of the mind, it is usually better to focus on singing devotional songs and chanting our mantra. Once we receive a mantra from a Satguru, a personal relationship is established between the Guru and ourselves. The mantra is the link that connects us with the Guru. This link or bond will last until we reach the goal — until we realize our Self.

Amma says that She has a connection with many of Her devotees from a previous birth. Her only purpose in incarnating Herself again and again on this earth is to help us reach the goal of human life. She doesn't have anything to gain; She has already gained everything there is to gain. We are very fortunate to have been initiated by a Spiritual Master like Amma.

The mantra is like a vehicle that will carry us to the goal much faster than if we had to walk the entire distance on foot. Before receiving a mantra, our spiritual progress might have been very slow and unsteady. When we receive mantra diksha, a portion of the Guru's prana shakti is transferred to us. After receiving that prana shakti, our spiritual progress will accelerate depending on the effort we put forth.

Some may ask, "Isn't chanting a mantra also just another thought in the mind? Then how can we achieve the state beyond thoughts?"

Amma says, "Through *japa* we can reduce the number of thoughts. When we put a sign on a wall that reads, 'stick no bills,' we prevent any other advertisements or graffiti from being written on the wall. Those three words get rid of hundreds of other words. Similarly, repeating the name of God with concentration reduces the number of other thoughts in our mind."

Even if we are not gaining concentration while chanting our mantra, we should continue to chant it. Amma says that the sound of the mantra contains positive spiritual vibrations that will have a beneficial effect on us regardless of our level of concentration.

When a Satguru like Amma gives a mantra, it comes with his or her powerful sankalpa that the mantra should benefit the receiver. The Satguru is making a commitment to lead us to the goal of human existence. To receive the maximum benefit, we have to reciprocate or respond with our own commitment — for our part, we should faithfully obey the Guru's instructions. ❖

CHAPTER 26

Three Ways Amma Protects Us

B ecause of the actions we have committed in the past, we are all destined to suffer in this life. Out of Her infinite compassion, Amma will shield us from our destiny to a great extent. Depending on the type of prarabdha giving rise to the experience, Amma will protect us in three different ways. She will completely protect us from an experience we were destined to have; She will give us partial protection, reducing the severity of the suffering we have to undergo; or She will give us the strength to undergo the experience. I have personally experienced all three kinds of help when faced with various difficulties in my life.

The first incident occurred when Amma, accompanied by the brahmacharis, was giving a series of programs in North Kerala. On our way from place to place, we would often stop near a river around dusk. We would all bathe and swim in the river. Then Amma would lead us in chanting the Gayatri mantra as we stood waist deep in the water. Sometimes we would also chant the 1,000 Names of the Divine Mother. Then we would meditate and sing bhajans on the shore as the sun went down. Finally, Amma would make tea for us before we continued on our journey. One evening after we had emerged from the river, I discovered I had lost my mala in the water. I was quite upset as the mala had been blessed and given to me by Amma. I also thought it might be a sign that something bad was going to happen to me. As soon as

I discovered it was gone, I ran to Amma's side and told Her what had happened. Immediately She took Her own mala from around Her neck and gave it to me. I was overjoyed by this unexpected blessing; this mala had been worn by Amma for quite some time. Not only that, the mala I had lost had only 54 beads, while the new one had 108. I gave no more thought to the original mala. I even thought it was a good thing that I had lost it in the river. We continued on our journey and finished the tour.

A few months later, I was going for my own tour, giving programs in Tamil Nadu. I was traveling by car with two other devotees. I was sitting in the back seat behind the driver. As we were on the way to the first program, a truck swerved out of the oncoming traffic and sideswiped our car at a very high speed. Both doors on the driver's side of the car were completely caved in, the windows were shattered, and glass shards were strewn everywhere. Of course, being inside such a massive vehicle, the truck driver was unharmed, but it was a miracle that all four passengers in our car emerged unscathed, especially considering the condition of the car after the accident.

I telephoned Amma as soon as I could to let Her know what had happened, and then, since no one had been hurt, I went along with the tour as planned. I returned to the ashram a month later. A few days after my return, I had a chance to see Amma in Her room. While I was sitting with Her and explaining the details of the accident, Amma was looking closely at the mala She had given me. I was wondering what She was doing when She suddenly told me to give the mala back to Her. I was shocked at Her request. Without returning the mala, I kept quiet. She again asked me to give it to Her. As I really did not want to give it up, I pleaded with Amma, saying, "Amma, after you have given a gift, it's not nice to ask for it back. You have so many other malas, what do you want with this one? Please let me keep this mala."

Amma again asked me to return the mala. "The mala I gave you has served its purpose. You don't need it anymore." Understanding that Amma was referring to the car accident, I gave the mala back to Her. In return, She gave me a different one to wear.

Of course, She did not need to give me a mala or any other object to protect me from harm. Her mere sankalpa would have been enough. She chose to protect me from this accident, and giving me the mala was Her spontaneous method to deliver this protection.

The second type of help or protection we can receive from a Satguru is a partial protection or a reduction in the severity of the suffering we have to undergo. Many years back, I used to drive the ashram van. When we were in Chennai, during the Tamil Nadu tour, I went to Amma's room to give Her something. As I stretched my arm to Her, She noticed a rash on my forearm. After inspecting the red spots, She told me I had chickenpox and that She would find someone else to drive for the rest of the tour, as She wanted me to go back to the ashram immediately. She added, "Don't worry, you won't really suffer from this illness."

The next day, when I went to take leave of Amma before going back to the Amritapuri ashram, She showed me Her arm. There was a rash there very similar to my own. "See," She said, "I have taken your chickenpox. You won't get any more chickenpox blisters."

Thus, I returned to the ashram while Amma and the other brahmacharis completed the tour. Around the same time, a few other people in the neighborhood of the ashram had contracted chickenpox, and they had developed blisters all over their body.

But after Amma told me that She had taken on my illness, I did not get even one more blister.

In the same way, Amma takes the illnesses of many others on Herself. When She gives darshan, She may take on the ailments of many people in a single day. I once asked Her, "Amma, how can you take so much sickness and pain on yourself? Don't you feel overwhelmed?" Amma responded that where someone else may have to suffer from a disease for 10 years, if She takes that disease on Herself, She can exhaust the same prarabdha in less than 10 minutes.

For every action that is performed, somebody must experience the result of that action. Normally, if we performed the action, we will experience the result. However, Mahatmas like Amma are able to take the results of the negative actions of many others on their own body, thereby exhausting our prarabdha and alleviating our suffering. In fact, Amma has even said that no matter the severity or the quantity of the prarabdha of others that She takes on Herself, She can burn it in the fire of Her Knowledge [12] in a single instant.

Two years ago, I had to undergo a knee operation. Previously Amma had told me it was a bad time for me, and I should be careful about my health. Because Amma did not specifically say what kind of health problem I should watch out for, I didn't worry about it. I just surrendered the problem — whatever it might be — to Amma. One day, shortly thereafter, I began to feel severe pain in my knees. When I told Her about it, Amma asked me to go to the hospital immediately. After examining me, the doctors

[12] Here Amma is referring to Brahmajnana, or the Knowledge of the omniscient, omnipotent, and all-pervading Brahman, the substratum of the universe. To gain this Knowledge means to become one with Brahman.

suggested I undergo corrective surgery. Even though it was to be a minor operation, I was feeling afraid because I had never had any serious injury or ailment in my life.

Amma told me I should undergo the surgery, so I made plans to go ahead with the operation. I was in the United States at the time, and I was so upset and scared about the impending operation that I would call Amma almost every day, praying to Her that She would somehow help me to avoid the surgery. Whenever I talked to Amma, She always reassured me, "Don't worry, my son, don't be afraid. Everything will be okay." Finally, the day of the scheduled operation arrived, and my condition had not improved, so I had no choice but to have the surgery. During the operation itself, I did not feel any fear at all. Afterward Amma told me that even though I had been unable to see Her, She had been there with me during the surgery. In this case, Amma did not help me in the way I expected; She did not remove the problem. Instead, She gave me the courage to face the experience with equanimity.

To give a more compelling example, once a man with two young children came for Amma's darshan in Australia. He told Amma his wife was suffering from terminal cancer, and she was vomiting blood and fainting frequently. Seeing their mother in this condition, their two little children, aged five and seven, at first became afraid and started crying. But after meeting Amma, there had been a change in their character. Their father had told them about how Amma would look after the sick and elderly when She was just a little girl, and the children had been inspired by Her example. Eventually, the children had come to terms with the situation and had even begun to take care of their mother. They would prop her up when she collapsed, bring her a glass of water and call the ambulance if necessary. They had become very strong and courageous.

"She wanted to come see Amma so badly," the man said about his wife, "but she is not even strong enough to walk, so she couldn't make it here tonight." When Amma heard their story, She poured endless motherly affection on them. She gave them so much attention, asking every little detail about their lives, playing with the children, asking about their studies, and hugging them repeatedly. All this happened in the midst of giving darshan to 1,000 people or more. In fact, Amma was so intent on showering love on this family, She wouldn't let them go. She acted as though She had all the time in the world. Finally, they took leave of Her, explaining their mother was waiting at home.

As he left, the father said, "Now I can face the suffering in my life. Amma has given my children and me the strength and love we need to overcome this challenge. Thank you so much." First by the example of Her life, and then by the love and affection She showed them personally, Amma helped this family to face an extremely challenging situation. Instead of being overcome by grief, they were able to help their mother and look after her every need.

Amma says there are three types of prarabdha. The first type is like a benign form of cancer — it can be completely removed by performing remedial actions such as spiritual practices and good deeds in conjunction with God's grace. The second type can be partially removed, but we will still have to suffer to some extent. It is like a cancer that can be treated but may return in the future. The third type is like a malignant cancer that cannot be removed — we just have to accept it. These three types of prarabdha correspond to the three types of help that Amma gives us. In situations arising from the third type of prarabdha (like a malignant, incurable form of cancer), Amma does not interfere with our prarabdha but allows it to run its course. This does not mean that Amma is abandoning us. When there is a painful experience that we have no choice but to endure, Amma gives us the strength to face the situation with courage and serenity. ❖

CHAPTER 27

Is Amma an Avatar?

According to Sanatana Dharma, when an ordinary person is born into the world, it is called *janma* (birth). Generally, it will not be the person's first birth, so it can also be called *punarjanma* (rebirth). However, when an enlightened person takes birth out of his or her own sankalpa in order to help others, he or she is referred to as an *Avatar*, or Incarnation. In many religions, believers accept only one person as an Incarnation of God. Sanatana Dharma is unique in that it recognizes many individuals as Avatars. Sanatana Dharma also declares unequivocally that God will manifest anywhere, at any time and in any form according to the situation prevailing at that time and the devotion of the devotees.

The Sanskrit word "avatar" comes from *ava-tarati* — to come down, assuming one body or another. This means that God, the Formless, comes down to our level, assuming a human form in the world of names and forms in order to lead us along the spiritual path. God does this to re-establish dharma for the maintenance of harmony and for the protection of the world.

In the *Bhagavad Gita*, Lord Krishna declares,

yadā yadā hi dharmasya glānir bhavati bhārata
abhyutthānam adharmasya tadātmānaṁ sṛjāmy aham

O Arjuna, whenever there is a decline in dharma
(righteousness) and an increase in adharma
(unrighteousness), I bring Myself into being (assume a
physical body). (4.7)

paritrāṇāya sādhūnāṁ vināśāya ca duṣkṛtām dharma-
saṁsthāpanārthāya sambhavāmi yuge yuge

For the protection of those who are committed to dharma,
for the destruction of those who follow adharma, and for
the establishment of dharma I am born in every age. (4.8)

When everything is going smoothly, there is no need for
an Avatar to come. It is only when chaos and confusion prevail
that the Lord comes. To give a more familiar example, when all
is peaceful in a neighborhood and there is no rioting or conflict,
the police force is not deployed. They come only when there is
a problem.

Sometimes, danger comes to dharma and upsets the harmony
of creation. Generally, the threat or violation comes only from
human beings. Plants and animals do not disturb the harmony of
creation, for they live their lives by natural instinct. Only human
beings violate this cosmic rhythm because of their arrogance, ego,
and lust for power.

When dharma is threatened, the Lord manifests as an Avatar.
To kill the demon Ravana, the Lord incarnated in a human form
as Rama. Ravana had received a boon that no demon, god, or
animal would be able to destroy him. Ravana had not asked for
protection from human beings because he thought no human
could harm him. Thus, the Lord manifested as a human being,

which was the only way to slay Ravana and re-establish dharma for that period.

Similarly, the demon Hiranyakasipu had received a boon that he could not be killed by any weapon, nor by a human being or an animal, in the day or night, on earth or in the sky, inside or outside his palace. In order to kill Hiranyakasipu, the Lord had to incarnate in the half-human, half-lion form of Narasimha and attack Hiranyakasipu at sunset (when it was neither day nor night). The Lord picked up the demon and placed him on his lap so that he was neither on the earth nor in the sky, carried him to the doorway of his palace so that he was neither inside nor outside, and killed him with his lion's claws (which, technically, were not weapons).

When an ordinary human being is born, it is because of two things. The first is his or her individual prarabdha. The second reason is the collective prarabdha of the world. The prarabdha of the world consists of large groups of individual prarabdhas. When the world is full of good, righteous people, it has good prarabdha resulting in peace and harmony. At a time when there are many unrighteous people causing problems for others, the world has bad prarabdha, and there will be violence and disharmony.

When the Lord or an already Self-realized Master is born in this world, it is not due to his or her own prarabdha but out of their sankalpa to help the world. Actually, Self-realized Masters do not have any prarabdha of their own. Prarabdha arises from the sense of doership, or the feeling that "I am doing." Ordinary human beings identify themselves with the body, mind, and intellect, rather than the Atman. According to Sanatana Dharma, this mistaken identification is called *avidya* (ignorance). Because we are ignorant of our True Self, when we perform an action, we will feel, "I have done this, and I want to get the result." Alternatively, if we do a bad thing, we will feel guilty or sorry for having done it. Either way, we will have to experience the result of our actions.

In truth, the Self, or Atman, does not do anything. It is actionless. That is why Self-realized Masters, who have realized their oneness with the Supreme Consciousness, know that they are not doing anything, but that everything just happens in their presence. Because of this knowledge, they do not have the feeling of doership. Thus, they cannot have any prarabdha of their own.

Why, then, do they appear? In the olden days, when an Avatar appeared, they killed the demons and the wicked people who had been torturing and killing good and innocent people. Thus, the Avatar could be considered the result of the good prarabdha of the righteous people in the world and the result of the bad prarabdha of the demons and unrighteous people. Krishna and Rama were kings, and it was their dharma to protect the nation from such wicked people. But Amma's dharma is different from that of a king. She sees Herself as the mother of all beings. Unlike Rama and Krishna, of course, Amma does not fight with anyone. Instead, through Her love and compassion, Amma is killing the wickedness within each of us.

According to the scriptures, there are certain characteristics that every Avatar will share. Such Great Souls do not harbor hatred toward anyone. Their teachings are universal. They will not reject even the greatest sinner. Without being attached to anyone, they love everyone equally. Leading a life of righteousness, they inspire others to follow their example.

Some might ask, if Amma is an Avatar, why doesn't She perform any miracles?

First, we must remember that a display of superhuman powers is not conclusive proof of an Avatar's identity. Certain Avatars, such as Lord Krishna, displayed superhuman powers. For example, in order to protect his childhood friends the gopas and gopis from torrential rain and lightning, he lifted Mount Govardhana and held it over their heads for seven days with only his smallest finger.

Even as a young child, Krishna killed quite a few powerful demons. The demon Ravana and all the other demons described in the epic Puranas also exhibited mystic or miraculous powers. On the other hand, other Avatars, such as Lord Rama, did not perform those kinds of superhuman powers. In fact, when Sita was kidnapped, Rama was searching for Sita and crying like an ordinary person. The exhibition of mystical or occult power cannot be considered conclusive proof in the determination of whether one is an Avatar.

That aside, those who ask why Amma doesn't perform miracles are missing the obvious: Amma's entire life is a miracle. There is so much we take for granted. During the last thirty years, Amma has individually given mantra initiation to millions of people, initiated thousands of brahmacharis and brahmacharinis into monastic life, and physically embraced more than 23 million people. She often embraces 20,000 or more people in a single day. When She travels in India, the numbers are much greater. On the last day of *Amritavarsham50*, Amma's 50th birthday celebration, She sat on the stage for nearly 24 hours and embraced more than 45,000 people. Finally, Amma left the stage not exhausted but with a beaming smile on Her face. How many people could we take on our shoulder before we collapsed with exhaustion? Also, this means that She sits in one spot for 15 to 20 hours a day. How many hours can we sit in one place? During this time, She does not even go to the bathroom.

When each person rests their head on Amma's shoulder, their face is so close to Her face that She is actually breathing their exhaled air — this happens thousands of times each day. Many doctors have said that if an ordinary person were to do this, they would contract terrible infections. Amma embraces people regardless of their cleanliness or state of health — She doesn't even hesitate to embrace lepers and people with other contagious skin diseases. Then, each and every person who comes to Amma wants to unburden their heart to Her. Even a trained psychologist can only listen to the problems of 10 or 20 people a day. Amma listens to the problems of thousands every day and shows equal love and attention to each person.

Many people are under the mistaken impression that when Amma finishes giving darshan for the day and goes to Her room, She will lie down and sleep. The truth is that when She is in Her room, She is as busy as ever. She makes an effort to read all of the letters She receives — hundreds each day. Unlike previous Mahatmas, Amma's activities are not confined to spirituality alone. Her activities extend to the fields of education, health, social, technological and environmental issues. She personally directs each of the humanitarian projects and educational institutions that Her ashram has founded. At the end of the day, She will lie down for just one or two hours. Who else can sleep so little and work so much?

Most people work eight hours a day, five days a week, and get two to six weeks of vacation a year. Amma works 20 hours a day or more and never takes a vacation. In the last 30 years, She has never taken a day off.

There is a bronze statue of Saint Peter in Rome. Pilgrims touch the statue's foot each day, and as a result, the left foot of the statue has been almost completely worn down. If just the light touch of the pilgrims can wear away a bronze statue, what should happen to a human being who has taken the full weight of so many millions?

We have not even begun to look at what She has accomplished on the social level. Is it not a miracle that this undereducated woman, with no financial support from business, global service organizations, government, political parties, or religious groups has established such a vast network of medical, educational, and service-oriented institutions within the last 15 years? In a world where women generally take a back seat, Amma has proven by Her example that for society to make real progress, men and women are as equally important as the two wings of a bird.

There are, of course, the well-known stories of the miracles Amma has performed — the healing of the leper Dattan with Her own saliva, the transforming of a small pot of ordinary water into enough *panchamritam* (sweet mixture of honey, milk, yogurt, clarified butter and sugar candy) to feed hundreds, using ordinary water to keep an oil lamp burning. [13]

In my association with Amma, whatever statements I have heard Her make about the future have always come to pass, no matter how unlikely they seemed at the time. When I met Amma 27 years ago, She told me that in the future, people from all over the world would come to Her and that She would travel all over the world to guide and console and comfort people. At that time,

---

[13] For more on these incidents, please refer to *Mata Amritanandamayi: A Biography* by Swami Amritaswarupananda Puri, or *Racing Along the Razor's Edge* by Swami Ramakrishnananda Puri.

there was not even one brahmachari staying with Amma. She did not even have a roof over Her head. She slept on the open ground in front of Her family's house. How could She have known that in the future such a vast network of spiritual and humanitarian activities would grow up around Her?

If we look closely at Amma's life, we would never ask where the miracles are, for they are everywhere, in every aspect of Her life. It would take volumes to list every miracle in Amma's life. Each of the millions who have encountered Amma will be able to share their own miraculous experiences—of character transformation, of the healing of inner wounds, of a "new lease on life," and yes, the unexpected healing of disease. This is an encyclopedia that will never be compiled on paper — it is written in the hearts of Amma's children.

Amma Herself has said, "I am not interested in making someone a believer by showing a miracle. My goal is to inspire people with the desire for liberation through realization of their Eternal Self. Miracles are illusory. They are not the essence of spirituality. Not only that, once a miracle is shown, you will demand to see one again and again. I am here not to create desire, but to remove it."

Sometimes, people accomplish nearly superhuman feats such as cycling extraordinary distances or standing on one foot for many hours, but it is only to get their name in the record books. Amma sets a world record anew each day, and yet She never gives a thought to what others say about Her — She is not doing what She does to receive praise but for the sake of the world. Once a journalist asked Amma, "Millions of people worship you as Devi. How does that make you feel?"

Amma replied, "I don't feel anything. People who call me Devi today may call me Devil tomorrow. It doesn't matter to me. I know who I am. I don't give importance to their praise or criticism. I flow like a river. People use it differently according to their nature. Some quench their thirst, some people sit on the banks enjoying the cool breeze, others will take a bath, and some may even spit in the river. But the river simply flows."

Amma tells us that She has always had the deep understanding that everything was God; on a few occasions, She has revealed that She was born enlightened. We also know that no one in the history of the world has ever done what Amma has done every day for the last 30 years, and no one has ever accomplished what She has accomplished. However, out of Her humility, Amma would never say that She is an Avatar. That is a question each of us will have to answer for ourselves. ❖

CHAPTER 28

You Have to Turn on the Light:
Grace & Effort

A devotee once asked, "Amma, if the soul is the same in all of us, then when one person realizes the Truth and becomes Self-realized, shouldn't everyone get Realization at the same time?"

Amma gave a beautiful reply. "Son, when you turn on the main power switch in the house, electricity reaches all the rooms — the living room, the kitchen, the bedrooms. However, if you want light in your room, you have to make the effort to turn the switch on in that room. Only if each person makes the effort and turns that switch on will the light inside be revealed."

Thus, it is up to us to do our part. We must put forward our best effort to advance along the spiritual path, sincerely performing our spiritual practices every day, trying to cultivate divine qualities like patience, acceptance, humility, and love, and following Amma's instructions.

We should never get discouraged in our efforts. As Amma says, "God's grace is the factor that governs all our efforts and makes all our actions sweet and complete."

There is a wonderful story that illustrates the complementary roles of our own efforts and the grace of God or Guru. Wishing to encourage her young son's progress on the piano, a mother took her boy to a concert where a world-renowned pianist was giving a performance. After they were seated, the mother spotted a friend in the audience and walked down the aisle to greet her. Seizing the opportunity to explore the wonders of the concert hall, the little boy rose and eventually explored his way through a door marked NO ADMITTANCE. When the houselights dimmed and the concert was about to begin, the mother returned to her seat and discovered that her child was missing.

Suddenly the curtains parted and the spotlights focused on the impressive piano on the stage. In horror the mother saw her little boy sitting at the keyboard innocently picking out "Twinkle, Twinkle Little Star." At that moment, the great maestro made his entrance. He quickly moved to the piano and whispered in the boy's ear, "Don't quit. Keep playing."

Then, leaning over, the maestro reached down with his left hand and began filling in a bass part. Soon his right arm reached around to the other side of the child and added to the music. Together the old master and the young novice transformed a frightening situation into a wonderfully creative experience, and the audience was mesmerized.

Similarly, whatever our situation in life, however outrageous, however desperate, whatever dry spell of the spirit, we can rest assured that Amma is whispering deep within us, "Don't quit. Keep playing. You are not alone. Together we will transform the broken patterns into a masterwork of creative art. Together we will mesmerize the world with our song." ❖

EPILOGUE

The Master's Love

"Just as fragrance cannot be separated from the flower, as light cannot be separated from fire, love and compassion cannot be separated from the Master."

—Amma

When Amma leaves the ashram, the road is always lined with devotees. When the car starts moving, Amma will roll down the windows and throw prasad candies out both sides of the car for all the people standing there — visiting devotees, ashram residents, even the neighboring villagers and their children.

Once when I was riding in the car with Amma, I noticed Amma was throwing these candies even after there were no more devotees lining the road but only villagers who were not interested in Amma's prasad. They just saw Amma and then left. They didn't even bother to pick up the prasad Amma had thrown. I told Amma, "All the devotees have taken Your prasad; from this point onward they are all just villagers. They just came out to the road to see what is going on. They are not picking up the prasad You are offering them."

"It doesn't matter," Amma replied. "If they don't take it, the children who come this way will take it. If the children don't take it, some animals will eat it or ants will eat it. Don't worry; it will not go to waste." Even if we don't appreciate it, even if we don't accept it, Amma still wants to shower Her love and affection on us.

Amma will always give us as much as She can — as much as time allows. Recently, when Amma came back to India after Her U.S. tour, about 14,000 people came for the first Devi Bhava darshan. Amma gave darshan from 7:30 p.m. to about 10:30 a.m. the next morning. Just a few days before, at the last Devi Bhava in the United States, the darshan began at 8:30 p.m. and ended at 11:00 a.m. Even though there were only about half the number of people, Amma took almost the same amount of time. She could have easily finished by 3:00 or 4:00 a.m. Instead, She chose to give more time to each person. She never thinks, "Oh! There are fewer people here; I can finish the darshan quickly and get some rest." If we had an opportunity like that, we would definitely take it, but Amma never does. She never wants to take a shortcut. She has shown time and again that She can embrace well over 1,500 people in an hour. But when She gives darshan to 750 people, She doesn't finish in half an hour — She takes just as long as if there were 10 times the number of people because She wants to give each person as much time as She possibly can.

Once, a mentally unbalanced man came for Amma's darshan with a bottle of something in his hand. Before we knew what he was planning to do, he had upended the bottle over Amma's head. Liquid perfume splashed over Amma's head and face and ran down into Her eyes. The other devotees were furious with the man and wanted to take him away from Amma, but She stopped them, saying he had done it only out of his devotion. She could not even open Her eyes because the chemicals in the perfume were burning so bad. Still, She was not angry with him. She knew that the man, in his unbalanced state, had not understood that it would be painful for Amma if he did such a thing. She even asked him to sit by Her side and consoled him as he was feeling very bad about his mistake.

What would we do in a similar situation? Seeing Amma's infinite patience, I was reminded of Her statement, "If we accidentally bite our tongue, we do not get angry at our teeth and break them off. We know that both tongue and teeth belong to us and are useful in their own ways. Similarly, Amma does not find anyone separate from Her. For Her, even the pain of an ant or a plant is as real as Her own suffering."

Amma suffers a great deal every day for the sake of Her children. When people come to receive Amma's darshan, many of them hold onto Amma very tightly, even digging their fingers into Her back or Her shoulder. But when anyone tries to remove the person's hand, Amma always stops them, saying the person will feel sad if we do not let them hold tightly to Amma. Other times people put all their weight on Amma's knees as they get up from receiving Her darshan, or they step on Her feet, or pull Her by the neck. When we ask Amma how She can tolerate all this physical abuse, Amma responds with a question, "Does a mother get angry at her child when it steps on her foot as it comes running to her lap?" Whether Amma is seeing us as Her children or as Her very own Self, Her love for us is infinite and unconditional.

Amma's love is not limited to human beings. Amma Herself tells a story from Her childhood that shows the depths of Her love and compassion for all beings in creation.

One day when Amma was young, She was waiting in line to collect water from the village tap when suddenly She felt a strong urge to return home. Without even waiting Her turn to fill Her buckets, She went home immediately. Even from a distance, She could see one of the family goats lying on the ground in its own waste, groaning in pain and frothing at the mouth. Amma rushed toward the dying animal and caressed it lovingly, whispering soothing words into its ear. Finally, She moved some distance away from the goat and sat down in meditation. When Amma opened Her eyes, She saw the goat laying with its head in Her lap. It had dragged itself with what must have been great difficulty across the yard to reach Amma where She was sitting. Amma caressed the goat's face again with great love and affection. Shortly, the goat breathed its last. Seeing its great effort to reach Her, Amma's heart melted. Out of Her infinite compassion, Amma bestowed liberation on the goat.

Through Her grace, even the goat in Her yard was able to achieve what humanity has always strived for.

What a great difference there is between our love and a Master's love. We may be able to love our family members and friends, even our neighbors. But we will not be able to love everyone. There may be somebody we dislike or even feel hatred toward. We, ourselves, know the limitations of our love.

Anyone who has met Amma knows Her love is different. Amma accepts all of us as we are; She does not reject anybody. Amma never says to a person, "You have a lot of negative qualities and bad habits. First remove your negativities and then come to me." Amma says that if She were to say that, it would be like a river saying to someone who was about to bathe in it, "Don't step into my waters; you are filthy and stinking with sweat. First clean yourself and then come and bathe here." Without taking a bath in the river, how is the person going to become clean?

One of Amma's American devotees used to be famous among the devotees for his short temper. Some years back, we were walking together alongside the orchard at Amma's ashram in San Ramon, California, and noticed a woman whom we didn't recognize plucking peaches from the trees and putting them in her bag. She was also holding some fruit in her hands as she started walking toward her car. As she was walking, a few peaches fell out of her hands and started rolling down the driveway. When the short-tempered devotee saw this, he ran down the driveway after the rolling fruits, picked them up, and lovingly placed them in the woman's bag. Witnessing the scene, I could not believe my eyes. In similar situations in the past, one could have seen this devotee shouting and chasing the "trespasser" off the ashram grounds. But on this occasion, the same person was chasing the peaches all the way down the hill, just to give them back to the woman who had taken them. Later, when I asked him about this, he said, "Oh, Swami, if this incident had happened a few years back, I would have scolded the woman for taking fruit that didn't belong to her. But after being with Amma for so many years, I cannot do anything other than what I did."

It is Amma's unconditional love that transformed this devotee and has transformed so many of Amma's children. We have been loved by our parents, friends, and spouse, but we have not been transformed by that love. It is the Master's love that transforms us.

The force of our old habits and vasanas make it difficult to practice positive qualities in our life. But Amma is so patient with us, so loving to us, She says She is ready to take any number of births for the sake of Her children. Moreover, She says She is ready to help us not only in this birth but in all our future births as well.

One day in Amritapuri, I went to the stage for the evening bhajans a little early. On the stage, I saw an earthen pot sitting in front of Amma's *peetham* (low platform on which She sits). I asked one of the brahmacharis who was setting up the stage, "What's the deal with the pot?" He told me that it was the ashes of a devotee of Amma who had recently passed away. I felt disgusted that the ashes of a dead person were being placed near where Amma was to sit. As I was brought up in an orthodox Brahmin tradition, I couldn't stand seeing a pot containing the ashes of a dead person near Amma's peetham, which I consider to be a temple. I immediately asked the brahmachari to move the pot somewhere else. I didn't want to touch the pot myself, as I considered it to be impure. The brahmachari politely declined, saying, "Swamiji, Amma wanted it on the stage."

"Then you can place it at the far end of the stage instead of right in front of Amma's peetham," I said. The brahmachari immediately did as I had asked.

After a few minutes, Amma came for the evening bhajans. After bowing down to the devotees, instead of sitting down immediately, She stood on Her peetham and started looking around the stage. When She spotted the pot containing the devotee's ashes, She immediately stepped off the peetham, walked to the pot, bent down and picked it up. She then turned and carried the pot back to Her peetham. I was surprised, even a bit shocked, that Amma would show so much respect for that pot of ashes. Because of my orthodox upbringing, I just could not understand Amma's action.

Amma kept the pot close to Her feet throughout the evening bhajans, sometimes even adjusting its position. I became increasingly restless. I started to feel guilty about my reaction, thinking it must be the ashes of a great devotee. After the bhajans, Amma stood up on Her peetham and bent down to pick up the pot. By that time, my attitude had changed completely; I was feeling remorseful for my earlier feeling toward the ashes. I immediately stood up and went to pick up the pot and hand it to Amma. As I was about to touch the pot, Amma stopped me and asked in a serious tone, "Why are you touching it now? Don't touch it." I felt as though a hammer had come down on my head. Again I tried to help Amma by lifting the pot, but She wouldn't let me. Picking up the pot Herself, She left the stage and began walking toward the beach to immerse the ashes in the ocean.

By then I was feeling terrible, thinking that I had been so disrespectful toward the last remains of a great devotee. I apologized to Amma and started walking along with Her. She told me not to follow Her and continued walking.

Soon thereafter, I got an opportunity to talk to Amma. I apologized to Her once again, and asked Her whose ashes had been in the pot.

Amma told me it was that of an elderly devotee who had long cherished the dream of performing Amma's pada puja. Before she had the opportunity, however, Amma went abroad for Her U.S. tour. The elderly woman consoled herself thinking she could do the pada puja when Amma returned from Her tour. But as fate would have it, the elderly woman passed away before Amma returned to India. A few days after Amma returned, the woman's son came to the ashram bearing the ashes of his mother. He gave the ashes to Amma, saying that his mother's dying wish was to bathe Amma's feet in the pada puja ceremony. He asked Amma to bless his mother's soul.

As soon as Amma heard this, She took the pot from the boy and held it close to Her heart, closing Her eyes for a few minutes. Then She told him to place the pot on the stage during the evening bhajans. Even though on that particular day, Amma was busy giving darshan and later meeting many visiting dignitaries, She did not forget to tell one of the brahmacharis to be sure that the ashes of the elderly devotee had been placed on the stage. Throughout the evening bhajans, Amma had kept the pot near Her feet, imagining the woman was doing the pada puja for Her.

"What a lucky devotee," I thought to myself. "What a compassionate Master."

Consider the depth of Amma's unconditional love. Amma could have simply blessed his mother's ashes and asked the son to immerse them in the ocean. Instead, She kept the pot with Her and showed so much respect and love for this devotee as to personally carry her ashes to the ocean. This shows how Amma is ready to fulfill our desires even after we leave the body. That is why Amma says, "Our own biological mother may take care of things we need in this birth, but Amma will take care of our needs not only in this birth but in all our future births too."

It is only a Mother's love for Her children that keeps Amma in Her body. Actually, She can discard the body any time She wants. Many years back, when I was talking to Amma one day, I spotted an insect crawling on Her head. When I tried to remove it, it went into Her hair and disappeared from view. I became concerned the insect might bite or sting Her, so I put my fingers into Her hair to take it out. As I was passing my fingers through Her hair, I was surprised to feel a very soft spot on the top of Her head. It was so soft that I felt that even a piece of Her skull might be missing. So, just to make sure Her skull was in proper condition, I again tried to feel that spot on the top of Her head.

At that point Amma pushed my hand away and said, "What are you doing?"

I said, "Amma, there's something wrong with Your head. I think a piece of Your skull is missing."

Amma replied, "Don't be foolish. There's nothing wrong with my skull. It's supposed to be like that."

"Why, Amma?" I asked. "My skull is hard as a rock."

Amma jokingly knocked on the top of my head, saying, "I will make it soft for you." Then, speaking seriously, She said, "That is the place through which the yogis withdraw their life-force when they exit this world. (She was referring to the *Brahmarandra*.) They can do it at any time they want and give up their body." I felt like a real fool, but I was amazed by Amma's answer. I had read about that in some books, but I had never seen any proof of it until that day. This shows us that Amma can leave Her body whenever She wants to. It is only out of Her overflowing love and compassion for us that Amma remains in the body—it is only to help Her children overcome their problems and reach the goal of human existence.

Amma is offering Her love to all of us, and that love has the power to heal all our inner wounds. It can transform anyone and everyone. Let us all try to be open to Amma's love. The more we are open to it, the more we will be transformed. ❖

Glossary

adharma – Unrighteousness. Deviation from natural harmony.

ahamkara – Ego or "the sense of a self existing separate from the rest of the universe."

Amrita Kuteeram – Mata Amritanandamayi Math's housing project providing free homes for very poor families. Over 30,000 houses have so far been built and given away throughout India.

Amritapuri –The international headquarters of Mata Amritanandamayi Math, located at Amma's birthplace in Kerala, India.

arati –Waving burning camphor before the image of the deity, normally signifying the closing of a ceremonial worship.

archana – Commonly refers to the chanting of the 108 or 1000 names of a particular deity (e.g. Lalita Sahasranama).

Arjuna –A great archer who is one of the heroes of the epic *Mahabharata*. It is Arjuna whom Krishna addresses in the *Bhagavad Gita*.

Ashtavakra Gita – "Song of Ashtavakra." It is the dialogue between King Janaka and the Master Ashtavakra on how to attain Knowledge of the Self.

Atman – The Self or Consciousness.

AUM – (Also "Om.") According to the Vedic scriptures, this is the primordial sound in the universe and the seed of creation. All other sounds arise out of Om and resolve back into Om.

Avatar – Divine Incarnation. From Sanskrit root "ava–tarati" — "to come down."

avidya – Ignorance that is the root cause of all sorrows.

Ayyappa –The presiding deity of the Sabarimala Temple in Kerala, considered as an Incarnation of Lord Shiva and Lord Vishnu.

Bhagavad Gita – "Song of the Lord." The teachings Lord Krishna gave Arjuna at the beginning of the Mahabharata War. It is a practical guide for facing a crisis in our personal or social life and is the essence of Vedic wisdom.

bhajan – Devotional song.

bhakti – Devotion, service and love for the Lord.

bhava – Mood or attitude (see Devi Bhava).

bhiksha – Alms.

Bhima – One of the Pandava brothers (see Pandavas).

bhogi – Enjoyer of sense pleasures.

bhuta yagna – Service rendered to and protection of other living beings.

Brahma yagna – Self-study, practice and teaching of spiritual scriptures.

brahmachari – A celibate male disciple who practices spiritual disciplines under a master. (Brahmacharini is the female equivalent.)

Brahmajnana – Knowledge of (direct experience of oneness with) Brahman.

Brahman – The Ultimate Truth beyond any attributes. Also, the omniscient, omnipotent, omnipresent substratum of the universe.

Brahmarandra – The subtle aperture at the top of the head through which the yogi withdraws his or her life force at the moment of physical death.

Brahmasthanam Temple – Born out of Amma's divine intuition, these unique temples are open to everyone irrespective of their religion. The central icon is four-sided, displaying Ganesha, Shiva, Devi and the Serpent, emphasizing the inherent unity underlying the manifold aspects of the Divine. At present, there are 17 such temples throughout India and one in Mauritius.

Brahmin – Priestly class of India.

Daksha – One of the prajapatis (progenitors) of humankind. Father of Shiva's bride, Sati. (See prajapati.)

darshan – An audience with a holy person or a vision of the Divine.

deva yagna – Worship of the presiding deities of the elements of nature.

devas – Celestial beings.

Devi – Goddess. The Divine Mother.

Devi Bhava – "The Divine Mood of Devi." The state in which Amma reveals Her oneness and identity with the Divine Mother.

dharma –In Sanskrit, dharma means "that which upholds (creation)." Most commonly, it indicates the harmony of the universe. Other meanings include: righteousness, duty, responsibility.

diksha – Initiation. Transfer of the seed of spiritual power (in a subtle form) from the Guru to the disciple.

Gayatri mantra – The mantra with which a person is initiated when he becomes qualified to be a Brahmin and is thereby authorized to conduct various yagnas.

gopa – The gopas were the cowherd boys; they were Krishna's childhood friends.

gopi –The gopis were milkmaids who lived in Brindavan where Krishna spent his childhood years. They were Krishna's ardent devotees. They exemplify the most intense love for God.

Hiranyakasipu –A demon who received a boon that he could not be killed by any weapon, nor by a human being or an animal, in the day or night, on earth or in the sky, inside or outside his palace. To circumvent the power of this boon, the Lord incarnated in the half-man half-lion form of Narasimha, laid Hiranyakasipu on his lap and killed him with his claws at dusk, while sitting in the doorstep.

irumudi – Bundle of coconuts, ghee and rice carried on the head by devotees of Lord Ayyappa on pilgrimage to Sabarimala.

janma – Birth.

japa – Repetition of a mantra.

jivanmukti – Liberation while still living in the body.

Jnani – A person who has realized God or the Self. One who knows the Truth.

karma – Conscious actions. Also, the chain of effects produced by our actions.

Kauravas –The 100 children of King Dhritharashtra and Queen Gandhari, of whom the unrighteous Duryodhana was the eldest. The Kauravas were the enemies of their cousins, the virtuous Pandavas, with whom they fought in the Mahabharata War.

Krishna – The principle incarnation of Vishnu. He was born into a royal family but grew up with foster parents and lived as a young cowherd in Brindavan where He was loved and worshipped by his devoted companions, the gopis and gopas. Krishna later established the city of Dwaraka. He was a friend and advisor to His cousins, the Pandavas, especially Arjuna, to whom He served as charioteer during the Mahabharata War, and to whom He revealed His teachings as the *Bhagavad Gita*.

Krishna Bhava – "The Divine Mood of Krishna." The state in which Amma revealed Her oneness and identity with Krishna. Initially, Amma used to give Krishna Bhava darshan immediately before giving Devi Bhava darshan. During Krishna Bhava, She did not identify with the problems of the devotees who came for Her darshan but remained as a witness. Deciding that the people of the modern world primarily needed the love and compassion of God as the Divine Mother, Amma stopped giving Krishna Bhava darshan in 1985.

Lalita Sahasranama – 1000 Names of the Divine Mother. Chanted daily at all of Amma's ashrams and centers and by devotees in groups and in individual homes.

lila – Divine play.

Mahabharata – One of the two great Indian historical epics, the other being the *Ramayana*. It is a great treatise on dharma. The story deals mainly with the conflict between the righteous

Pandavas and the unrighteous Kauravas and the great war at Kurukshetra. Containing 100,000 verses, it is the longest epic poem in the world, written around 3,200 B.C. by the sage Vyasa.

mahati vinashti – Literally, "the great loss." Refers to the failure to realize the Self during one's lifetime.

Mahatma – Literally, "Great Soul." Though the term is now used more broadly, in this book Mahatma refers to one who abides in the Knowledge that he or she is one with the Universal Self, or Atman.

mala – Rosary.

mantra diksha – Initiation by mantra.

Mata Amritanandamayi Devi –Amma's official monastic name, meaning Mother of Immortal Bliss, often prefixed with Sri to denote auspiciousness.

mithya – Changing, therefore impermanent. Also, illusory or untrue. According to Vedanta, the entire visible world is mithya.

naimithika karma – Rituals to be performed on special occasions, such as marriage, death, etc.

nara yagna – Service to our fellow human beings

Narasimha – Half–lion, half–human incarnation of Vishnu. (See Hiranyakasipu.)

nayana diksha – Initiation by glance.

nishiddha karma – Actions prohibited by the scriptures.

nitya karma – Actions to be performed daily, as per the scriptural injunctions.

Om Amriteswaryai Namah – Mantra that devotees use to honor Amma, meaning, "Salutations to the Goddess of Immortality (Amma)."

Om Namah Shivaya – Powerful mantra meaning, "I bow down to the Eternally Auspicious One."

pada diksha – Initiation by touch of the foot.

pada puja –Ceremonial washing of the Guru's feet, or his or her sandals, as a demonstration of love and respect. Usually includes the pouring of pure water, milk, yogurt, ghee, honey and rose water.

panchamahayagna –The Five Great Sacrifices that a householder should observe daily to repay our indebtedness to nature and the natural forces.

panchamritam –Sweet mixture of honey, milk, yogurt, clarified butter and sugar candy.

Pandavas –Five sons of King Pandu and the heroes of the epic, the *Mahabharata.*

Parvati – Consort of Lord Shiva.

peetham – Low platform. Seat for the Guru.

pitr yagna – Rituals performed for departed ancestors.

pitr loka – World of the departed.

prajapati – The first born from whom all other creatures, including human beings, demons and celestial beings, were born.

prana shakti – Vital force.

prarabdha   The fruits of actions from previous lives that one is destined to experience in the present life.

prasad – Blessed offering or gift from a holy person or temple, often in the form of food.

prayaschitta karma – Remedial actions. Performed to eliminate the negative results of previous actions which were intentionally harmful.

preyo marga –Pursuit of material happiness, e.g. wealth, power, fame.

puja – Ritualistic or ceremonial worship.

punarjanma – Rebirth.

Puranas – Through concrete examples, myths, stories, legends, lives of saints, kings and great men and women, allegories and chronicles of great historical events, the Puranas aim to make the teachings of the Vedas available to all.

Rahu – Refers to an eclipse of the sun by the moon. Considered as a shadow planet in Vedic astrology.

Rakshasa – Demon.

Rama – The divine hero of the epic Ramayana. An incarnation of Lord Vishnu, he is considered the ideal of dharma and virtue.

Ravana – Powerful demon. Vishnu incarnated as Lord Rama for the purpose of slaying Ravana and thereby restoring harmony to the world.

rishi – Self–realized seers or sages who perceive the mantras.

Sabarimala – Temple dedicated to Lord Ayyappa located at Western Ghats in Kerala.

sadhana – Spiritual practice.

samadhi – Oneness with God. A transcendental state in which one loses all sense of individual identity.

samsara – The cycle of birth and death.

Sanatana Dharma – "The Eternal Way of Life." The original and traditional name for Hinduism.

sankalpa – Divine resolve.

sannyasin – A monk who has taken formal vows of renunciation (sannyasa). A sannyasin traditionally wears an ochre–colored cloth representing the burning away of all desires. The female equivalent is a sannyasini.

Satguru – Literally, "True Master." All Satgurus are Mahatmas, but not all Mahatmas are Satgurus. The Satguru is one who, while still experiencing the bliss of the Self, chooses to come down to the level of ordinary people in order to help them grow spiritually.

Sati – Daughter of Daksha, bride of Shiva. Unable to bear Daksha's criticism of Shiva, Sati immolated herself through yogic fire drawn up from within herself. Later she was reborn as Parvati and became the consort of Shiva.

satsang – Being in communion with the Supreme Truth. Also being in the company of the Mahatmas, listening to a spiritual talk or discussion, and participating in spiritual practices in a group setting.

seva – Selfless service, the results of which are dedicated to God.

Shankaracharya – Mahatma who re–established, through his works, the supremacy of the Advaita philosophy of non–duality at a time when Sanatana Dharma was on the decline.

Shiva – Worshipped as the first and foremost in the lineage of Gurus, and as the formless substratum of the universe in relationship to the creatrix Shakti. He is the Lord of destruction in the trinity of Brahma (Lord of creation), Vishnu (Lord of preservation), and Shiva. Usually depicted as a monk, with ash all over his body, snakes in his hair, wearing only a loincloth and with a begging bowl and a trident in his hands.

Sita – Rama's holy consort. In India, she is considered to be the ideal of womanhood.

smarana diksha – Initiation by thought.

sparsha diksha – Initiation by physical touch.

sreyo marga – The pursuit of ultimate happiness, i.e. Self-realization.

Sudhamani – Amma's name, given by her parents at the time of birth, meaning, "Ambrosial Jewel."

tapas – Austerities, penance.

Tiruvannamalai – Town at the foot of the sacred Arunachala hill in the South Indian state of Tamil Nadu. The famous saint, Ramana Maharshi, lived there.

tattva bhakti – Devotion based on knowledge, or right understanding, of the Guru's or God's real nature.

Upanishads – The portions of the Vedas dealing with the subject of Brahman, the Supreme Truth and the path to realize that Truth.

vairagya – Detachment. Especially detachment from all that is impermanent, i.e. the entire visible world.

vasana – Latent tendency or subtle desire within the mind which manifests as action and habit.

Vedanta – "The end of the Vedas." It refers to the Upanishads. (See Upanishads.)

Vedas – Most ancient of all scriptures, the Vedas were not composed by any human author but were "revealed" in deep meditation to the ancient rishis. The mantras comprising the Vedas always existed in nature in the form of subtle vibrations; the rishis attained such a deep state of absorption that they were able to perceive these mantras.

vedic – Of or pertaining to the ancient Vedas.

vibhuti – Holy ash (often sanctified by the Guru's blessing).

viveka – Discrimination. Especially discrimination between the Permanent and the impermanent.

yagna – Sacrifice, in the sense of offering something in worship or performing an action for personal as well as communal benefits.

yoga – "To unite." Union with the Supreme Being. A broad term, it also refers to the various practical methods through which one can attain oneness with the Divine. A path that leads to Self-realization.

yogi – A practitioner or an adept of yoga.

www.ingramcontent.com/pod-product-compliance
Lightning Source LLC
Chambersburg PA
CBHW071212090426
42736CB00014B/2795